Presented ⟨ W9-DJF-854
to Lyle McCormick
by the pre-School
department of the
Methodist Sunday School

MAN TO MAN

by

Richard C. Halverson

Cowman Publications, Inc.
Los Angeles 38, California

Printed and Bound by Rand McNally and Co.

To

L. David Cowie, who introduced me to Christ, and whose early care and counsel cast my life in the mold of Romans 12: 1 and 2.

MAN TO MAN

"Blessed is the man that walketh not in the
counsel of the ungodly, nor standeth in the way
of sinners, nor sitteth in the seat of the scornful.
But his delight is in the law of the Lord; and in
His law doth he meditate day and night. And he
shall be like a tree planted by the rivers of water,
that bringeth forth his fruit in his season; his leaf
also shall not wither; and whatsoever he doeth
shall prosper . . . . ."

Psalm 1:1-3

Prologue

Man out of touch with God is a caricature!

Man out of fellowship with God is man out of place!

As the fish was made for water, man was made for God. In God man "lives and moves and has his being." God is the *native habitat* for which man was created, in which man was intended to dwell. The fish may be active as it flops and wiggles on the shore, but it is doomed. It is just a question of time. And man, individually and collectively out of fellowship with God may be very active, *but he has no future!*

Man was meant to be free, gloriously free, the servant of God alone. Man enjoys his maximum freedom—his optimum productivity and efficiency, when he serves God. Mastered by God, man is the master of himself and his world. Mastered by something less than God, man is the victim of himself and his world. He may think he is having his own way, but it is sheer illusion, his freedom is increasingly restricted until he is enslaved by an environment he was intended to master. He becomes less and less the man God intended him to be, more and more conscious of what he is missing in life, more and more aware of his bondage to habits which were begun in the name of Liberty. He finds himself less and less in control, more and more dominated by circumstances beyond his control.

Man must be ruled by God or he will be enslaved by tyrants!

Man was made for God and his restlessness increases in ratio to his rebellion against the rule of God in his life until rebellion leads to total impasse and man finds himself arriving at the ultimate in frustration and futility. (This in fact is collective man at the mid-twentieth century.)

As man takes God seriously and gives himself to God, he grows, matures, expands into progressively greater freedom, efficiency, productivity, fulfillment; as man resists God, life becomes increasingly confining.

Man without God experiences an increasing hunger that finds less and less satisfaction in life. Satisfaction comes in inverse ratio to his effort to find it. He learns more and more about less and less, becomes increasingly insensitive to the basic realities of life, increasingly immune to the deep things of the heart and mind, increasingly impervious to the loving overtures of God in Christ. He ends up with an insatiable appetite that gnaws and growls interminably. *He is God hungry!*

Rejecting God from his life, man sets himself on a road that leads to ever-increasing dissatisfaction, frustration and emptiness. He becomes a hollow soul, a bubble, a zero with the edges rubbed off, a meaningless cipher in a mass of meaningless ciphers. The life that defects from God is a life of drift, meaningless, purposeless, directionless.

The most predictable thing in life is sin and the worst sin is self-alienation from God whether by militant revolt or quiet, respectable indifference. Sin leads to boredom, total boredom. The more a man sins, the less he gets out of it, until he goes all the way and receives nothing. Sin numbs a man, renders him totally insensitive to its effects, and totally vulnerable to its devices. Sin takes the shine and vitality and virility out of life. It is dulling, enervating, debilitating. Sin is like quicksand. The more a man struggles once he is in its grip, the deeper he sinks helplessly into it.

Skidrow is the end of the line in miniature for the sinner. The hopelessness, colorlessness, shallowness, the sheer boredom and drift of skidrow is a candid shot of the pay-off of sin in this world. The important thing to remember is that a man can be on skidrow figuratively, if not literally. He may have enough money, position, prestige to keep himself off the street and out of the gutter, but the only difference is one of geography. He is as much a skidrow bum as the little fellow the cops pick up perennially and throw into the tank or boot out of town as a vagrant.

"Thou has made us for Thyself O God,
And restless are our hearts until they rest
in Thee."   —St. Augustine

"For the wages of sin is death, but the gift
of God is eternal life through Jesus Christ
our Lord."
                         Romans 6:23

Contents

CONTENTS

CONTENTS

11

CONTENTS

The Man's Man

CHAPTER

ONE

Man At His Best

The Man's Man

Ephesians 4:17-32

Man was made "in the image of God." Obviously the more God-like man is, the more man-like he will be, and conversely, the less like God he is, the less of a man he is!

One of the most insidious, diabolical lies ever perpetrated on humanity is the insinuation that God-likeness means shallow, blue-nosed piety. Jesus was perfectly God-like, and He was a man of men, a man in the fullest sense of the word, a perfect man. In fact, He was the only *normal* man who ever lived.

Man out of fellowship with God is sub-normal, Jesus Christ was normal.

But he was not pious in the accepted sense of that word today. On the contrary, He upset all the concepts of piety held by his contemporaries. He was continually breaking their rules. They labeled Him a "drunkard, glutton, winebibber." He drew His greatest hostility from the most religious.

In the strictest sense of the word, the grace of God works in man to make him more like Jesus. It might be said that the goal of the heavenly Father in the life of the Christian is to make him like His Son. As the process of becoming more like the Son of God develops in a man, he grows in manliness.

This is a basic paradox, that the more like Jesus a man is, the more manly he will be, and the less like Jesus, the less of a man he is. The measure of manhood is the measure of a man's Godliness. As God created man originally, only God can fashion manhood.

It takes God to make a man! Wise therefore the man who consents to the Father's will, who yields to the daily ministry of the Holy Spirit in conforming him into the likeness of Christ. "We all, with unveiled face, beholding the glory of the Lord, are being changed into His likeness . . ."—2 Corinthians 3:18 (RSV)

✣✣✣✣✣✣✣✣✣✣✣

Paul's analysis of the unregenerative man in verses 17–19 is very specific. What are the characteristics of this so-called "Gentile walk?" What is the significance of verses 22–24? Note the office of the Holy Spirit as suggested in verse 30 and the Apostle's warning.

15

Christian, not by encouraging himself to believe that things will be better tomorrow, but by reminding himself of the integrity and faithfulness of God. The Christian does not draw strength from circumstances, he draws strength from the living God. Actually, *holiness means wholeness*, inward health. That man is sickly, however strong his body, whose soul is uncared for.

The Peril Of Idolatry

Jeremiah 2:5-13

Here is one of the most pathetic questions ever put to man. God is the inquirer, and in essence He is saying, "What's the matter with me that my people have turned their backs on me and gone after idols?" Following the question He reminds them of His goodness and provision. Then He pleads with them to consider other nations, Godless nations, who are idolaters. These idolatrous nations are faithful to *their* idols and consistent with *their* beliefs. Only the people of God forsake their Lord.

The query is timely. The western civilization we enjoy today is the fruit of a Judea-Christian tradition —a faith which made men strong and courageous and free. The root is faith in God and in His Son, the Lord Jesus Christ. But we in the west have forsaken God. Not theoretically, for we still say we believe in Him, and we pay Him lip service. But we leave Him out of our plans. We live as though God was meant only for Sunday morning. We have become preoccupied with the idols of success or fame or wealth or popularity or prestige and status.

Meanwhile consider the nations that have no God. Consider the atheists. They are true to their No-God. They have not forsaken their beliefs. They are dedicated to their faith and they have a pioneering zeal that makes our Western world seem soft and fat and lazy.

We cannot have the fruit without the roots. We forsake the benefits ultimately if we reject the One Who is the Source of those benefits. "For my people have committed two evils; they have forsaken me the fountain of living waters, and hewed them out cisterns, broken cisterns, that can hold no water." —Jeremiah 2:13.

❖❖❖❖❖❖❖❖❖❖❖

Two inviolate principles of life are implicit in Jeremiah 2:5: First, man is incurably religious. He must have a true God or a substitute. The man who turns from God will find himself serving one idol or another. This is inevitable. Even the atheist has a faith. He believes in No-god! And the sincere atheist is often more religious than the Christian. Man's spirit abhors a vacuum and must have something or someone in which to believe.

Either man will worship God, or he will embrace false beliefs.

Second, man becomes like the god he worships. Man grows into the image of the true God when he follows Him, or he is molded into the shape of the idol which replaces God in his life.

Destiny In An Infant

Luke 2:22-35

One of the things about the Christian solution that commends it to thoughtful men is its uninventability. That's a big word which simply means that the Christian answer is so completely unlike man's way of doing things—so utterly contrary to human wisdom—that it must have come from somewhere else ... from God, for example.

Take Christmas as an illustration. Only God could have thought of that! When man wants to invent a super-being with superhuman powers, he produces a Superman or Captain Marvel. *But God gave the world a baby!* And in that infant was tied up the whole destiny of the world and history and mankind. That is the staggering theme of the Bible.

The Bible is the revelation of God's plan, conceived before history began and consummated after history is finished, but running through history and involving history's men and empires. God is at work in history, through history, to bring to pass His eternal purpose. But the amazing thing is the fact that this whole eternal program centers in a baby! Who ever would have thought of that? It is outside the realm of human inventiveness.

Inasmuch as God's purposes are bound up in and worked out through His Son Jesus Christ, every man becomes his highest and noblest self in right relation to Jesus Christ. A man's relationship to Christ is absolutely paramount if that man intends to make the most of life. "For God has allowed us to know the secret of His plan, and it is this; He purposes in His sovereign will that all human history shall be consummated in Christ; that everything that exists in heaven or earth shall find its perfection and its fulfillment in Him."—Ephesians 1:9-10.[1]

✦✦✦✦✦✦✦✦✦✦✦✦

What does Jesus Christ mean to you? What significance, if any, does the central fact of Christmas have in your life?

[1] J. B. Phillips, *The New Testament In Modern English* (New York: Macmillan Company, 1958)

Divine Diagnosis

Mark 7:14-23

Accurate diagnosis is fundamental to a cure. However excellent the prescription, it is inadequate for healing if based on incorrect analysis of the symptoms. This is the explanation for the monotonous, aggravating failure of man's best efforts to solve his problems. This is the perplexing dilemma of modern man. He's operating on a faulty diagnosis!

Human nature being what it is and human pride persisting as it does, man refuses to believe anything but the best about himself. ("There's so much good in the worst of us and so much bad in the best of us, that it hardly behooves any of us, to talk about the rest of us.") With arrogant impunity he relegates realism to the limbo of pessimism, taking comfort from the illusion that there is nothing wrong with human nature that a little more education and science —and the right political party in power will not solve, given a little time.

Human-like, man blames everything but himself for his trouble. It's the government or education or economics or the military or the law or management or labor or capital or preachers or the Church or Protestants or Catholics or Jews or religion or teachers or Congress or the Supreme Court or newspapers or Wall Street or Krushchev or Communism, and so on, ad-nauseum.

Everything is wrong except man himself!

So man goes on in his blundering, egotistical way puttering with the symptoms while the disease rages unchecked. The pay-off is precisely what we feel at the mid-twentieth century—complete frustration. Take a frank look at our position in this enlightened age . . .

We are more knowledgeable about child psychology than we've ever been, yet juvenile delinquency steadily increases.

Law enforcement has become an exact science and sociologists have produced the answers on rehabilitation of the criminal, yet the crime rate rises every year.

Elaborate, scholarly research has gone into alcoholism and its causes. A. A. labors tirelessly around the clock, yet in the United States there are fifty new alcoholics every hour (1200 a day).

Books and articles by the hundreds are published

on marriage and the home, marriage clinics and coun-
sellors abound everywhere, yet the divorce rate
ascends inexorably.

In an era of unprecedented application of psychology, psychiatry, psychoanalysis, and psycho-
therapy, mental hospitals are bulging, mental illness
is skyrocketing, and millions exist on Benzedrine,
tranquilizers and sleeping pills. Even the perfecting
of astounding new antibiotics seems to trigger new,
unfamiliar and mystifying virus.

While America is burdened with a growing food
surplus, half the world never knows the luxury of
a full stomach and millions perish of starvation annually—and apparently the only solution man can
devise for the dreaded population explosion is some
method of preventing babies from being born.

Diplomacy has become a profession, if not a fine
art. In high optimism, the United Nations was born
out of the disillusionment of an abortive League of
Nations, nevertheless, international relations are
more precarious and explosive than at any other time
in history. Two world wars have been fought in a
quarter-century, yet, despite earnest, unceasing
efforts at disarmament, these ensues an almost hys-
terical race to stock-pile mass-suicidal weapons.

There is more and more talk about peace—and
less and less hope for it . . .

All humanity longs and struggles for freedom, yet

half the world languishes under two giant dictator-
ships and a host of lesser ones—and the monolith of
communism, like a juggernaut, rolls over the world.
Science has united the world as never before, made
the dream of one world a more realistic hope than
it has ever been, yet the world has never been so
divided and fragmented: two Germanies, two Ko-
reas, two Chinas, two Viet-nams, an amazing birth
rate of newly independent states—and tighter and
tighter lines between the blacks, the browns, the
yellows, and the whites.

Incredible progress has been made in science and
technology, but the consummate product of that
progress constitutes a sickening, relentless threat to
the survival of civilization. Meanwhile human nature
sweats it out, blaming everything but itself for its
confusion and perplexity.

One step forward and two backward, seems to be
the pattern of history. It looks like the smarter we
are, the farther behind we get—the more we know,
the less we can do about it!

However, the mystery lifts when we consider the
diagnosis Jesus made as it is recorded in Mark 7:14-
23. *He declared that the trouble lay within human
nature itself.* He diagnosed it as a malignancy in the
human heart which infects all that man does. Man's
trouble originates *within* man, springing from a con-

dition in his nature which only God is adequate to meet. The burdens of the world are the symptoms of which the disease is sin, and the only cure for sin is the redemption that is in Jesus Christ.

Not the way human nature is organized, but human nature itself is the root of the problem. In the words of Dr. Louis H. Evans, Minister at large for the United Presbyterian Church, U. S. A., "It doesn't make any difference how cleverly you arrange bad eggs, you can't make a good omelet." While he was president of the United Nations General Assembly, General Carlos Romulo of the Philippines, said, "We have harnessed the atom, but we will never make war obsolete until we find a force that can bridle the passions of men and nations." This is the big question, where do we find that force?

The answer is the Gospel of Jesus Christ which is "the power of God unto salvation to every one that believeth, to the Jew first and also to the Greek." —Romans 1:16.

❋❋❋❋❋❋❋❋❋❋❋❋

Don't sell Christianity short! There is not a problem besetting the world today, nor has there ever been, that does not have its solution in Jesus Christ and His Gospel. Christendom has failed, the Church has failed, Christians have failed, but Jesus Christ will not fail, and as the world and the Church take Him seriously and look to Him for the answer, the dreams for which the whole created universe languish will be forthcoming.

Jesus Christ is the Lord of the universe. Jesus Christ is the Lord of History. Let Jesus Christ be your Lord and let His solution for man begin with you, now!

Christ's Cause

John 12:27-36

Why didn't Jesus wipe out human misery 1900 years ago?

According to the record He gave sight to three blind men, why not eliminate blindness? He touched cripples and they walked, He made the deaf to hear, the dumb to speak—why not do this for all cripples, all who are deaf or dumb? He cleansed lepers, why not rid the world of disease? He fed thousands with a few scraps of food, and there were basketfulls left over—why should anyone have to go hungry? For that matter, the record says He raised three people from the dead—why not bring everyone back to life, cancel out death completely?

Had Jesus reached the limits of His power? Did He handle as many cases as He was capable of handling, have to leave the rest to their misery? Or did He become indifferent finally—did He just lose interest in men's need? He said, "No man takes my life from me, I lay it down of myself, I take it up again. I have the power to lay it down and take it up again." If so, why did He allow Himself to be crucified? Why didn't He stay alive, eliminate sickness, disease, poverty, misery and death in His generation, and permanently?

Because He was the Great Physician! *He knew man's misery is a symptom.* He knew the disease itself was sin, and the only cure for sin was the shedding of blood. His mission was the cross. His cure for the disease was the sacrifice of His own blood. He was born to be crucified!

Thank God for medical science that refuses to be satisfied simply with treatment that helps man endure illness, that does not rest until it finds a cure. Iron lungs are fine, but how grateful we ought to be that medical science will never stop until it finds a cure for polio.

Jesus could have dealt only with the symptoms, kept pumping life and health back into man generation by generation ad-infinitum, but so what? He came to cure the disease of sin altogether, to eliminate the virus, so man would no longer be infected by it ever!

He did precisely that! That is the whole point of His birth, His life, His teaching, His death . . . His resurrection. He is God's eternal answer, God's

31

once-for-all-cure for man's deepest need. Of course a cure won't work unless a man takes it. Obviously! What pathetic absurdity to see man still preoccupied with the symptoms, still trying to solve his sociological problems while he ignores the affliction that produces them. "Behold the Lamb of God that taketh away the sin of the world!"

❖❖❖❖❖❖❖❖❖❖❖

Jesus was not martyred. Death did not overtake Him. His mission in the world was crucifixion. Read Peter's statement as he preached on Pentecost, Acts 2:22-23. Notice verses 31-33 of the passage under consideration.

Haste Makes Waste

Haste in the name of urgency may be deceptive, may indicate a lack of balance between awareness of the need and confidence in God's adequacy.

One can examine with meticulous care the New Testament record of Jesus' life without finding any evidence of hurry on His part. And He knew He had but three years to fulfill His mission. His concern for the need of man was unequalled. His total conformity to the will of the heavenly Father was indisputable. He knew the world of His time better than any contemporary. He was aware more than any other of the desperate need for divine intervention, yet His life was characterized in the words of one devotional writer, by "exquisite leisure."

Jesus never wasted time, but He never allowed Himself to be pressed into panic either. He knew the abysmal need for the light and life and love of God in the world better than any other man before or since His time, but He enjoyed complete confidence in the providential, over-arching care of Almighty God and the perfection of His plan in history. Jesus was delicately sensitive to the human dilemma; He was likewise sublimely relaxed in the Will of God. He bore man's burdens, shared man's suffering as no other, but He trusted implicitly in the Father's timing.

Our day demands greater emulation of our Lord in this respect. This does not justify laziness or apathy, which are inexcusable for the Christian, but it does urge deeper confidence in God's faithful and unfailing love.

Give us men, who, realistically awake to the explosive issues and are alert to their obligation, nevertheless demonstrate unbending faith in the unalterable integrity of God. Such men will not be in a hurry! But they will deliver the goods to the right place in the right way at the right time. With feet on the ground, their hearts in touch with heaven, they will be God's appointed men for God's appointed hour! "He that believeth shall not make haste."—Isaiah 28:16.

* * *

What do you take James to mean by his statement in verses 6, 7 and 8?

Grace To Receive

John 15:1-11

Sometimes the hardest thing a man does is accept a gift. Conditioned from childhood to be self-reliant, he gets the idea that anything he doesn't pay for is charity, and charity is a disgrace. Strongly indoctrinated with what William H. Whyte, Jr. (THE ORGANIZATION MAN) calls "the protestant ethic," he goes for "rugged individualism" with a strong dose of "there's plenty-of-room-at-the-top" philosophy. Being a self-made man is the mark of success, so the hard-headed businessman is inclined to treat with contempt anything that comes easy or has no price tag attached. Paying his own way is almost an obsession, and he prides himself on the fact that he's had to "go it alone," and what he has was hard come by. He enjoys a rather smug satisfaction in the blood, sweat and tears of attainment.

Which is right as far as it goes, but it can be pushed beyond virtue. Satisfaction in accomplishment may be replaced by conceit. Pride can turn the merit of achievement into the demerit of egotism, which will deprive a man of some of life's greatest benefits. A man can become so wrapped up in himself (this makes a small package) that he becomes insensitive to the benevolence about him which was meant for him to accept and enjoy without price.

There's no price tag on the beauties of nature: the simmering mystery of desert vastness; the tranquil majesty of the mountain; the dynamic silence of a stream whose cool depths are alive with flashing, glittering trout; the pristine glory of a sunrise; the flaming beauty of a sunset; the uncountable, immeasureable, indescribable luxury God has lavished on the world. It is as free as the air to all who take it. Nobody can get a corner on it. It belongs to everybody.

Even love, which, incidentally cannot be bought, may become meaningless to a man who forgets how to receive.

Worst of all, such a philosophy may deprive a man of the supreme gift of God which is eternal life through His Son. Eternal life is a gift, it cannot be purchased, nor will it ever be deserved. *It is free, but it is not cheap!* It cost God the priceless gift of His Son on the cross, the costliest gift ever offered.

Pity the hard-headed businessman who has let

drive and self-reliance go to his head and close the door of his heart upon the greatest asset of all, eternal life through Jesus Christ. "For God so loved the world that He gave His only begotten Son, that whosoever believeth on Him should not perish but have everlasting life."—John 3:16.

❖❖❖❖❖❖❖❖❖❖❖

The average businessman would do well to read John 15:1-11 every day of his life. The last statement in verse 5 is worth everything to a man when the truth of it finally sinks in. In the context of this passage, take a look at John 3:27 and 1 Corinthians 4:7 and James 1:16-17. Where does the life of the branch come from? For that matter, how did you become alive? What did you have to do with getting your life originally?

CHAPTER TWO

The Man Who Knows
Where He Is Going

Better Than A Known Way

Psalm 32:1-8

Only a fool would set out on an unknown way without a navigator. Without direction, man drifts.

The fact that God takes a personal, detailed interest in anyone who takes Him seriously is one of the most obvious truths in the Bible. God has a plan for every man who is willing to be led. God delights in making His way known and directing a man step by step in that way.

But God cannot force His will upon man. God works in and for man only as man consents. Nothing is more reasonable than that a man go God's way . . . nothing is more irrational than for a man to refuse God's way and grope into the future.

Abraham went out "not knowing whither he went" but he discovered that trusting God was better than a known way and a well charted course. Put your hand in God's and walk into the future with confidence. "By faith Abraham obeyed when he was called to go out to a place which he was to receive as an inheritance; and he went out, not knowing where he was to go."—Hebrews 11:8. (R.S.V.)

✸✸✸✸✸✸✸✸✸✸✸

Consider well the alternatives to a God-directed life. Psalm 32 is filled with remarkable provisions which God has made for the man who seeks Him.

More Than Conquerors

Romans 8:28-39

"Radar equipped" stands for the ultimate in air-travel safety. It guarantees the smoothest possible flight—gives the maximum assurance of arrival at destination, regardless of weather. Radar doesn't eliminate bad flying conditions, but it enables man to fly without being their victim. The weather is there, but a man can fly above or around it and land safely.

A man may ignore radar as though it doesn't exist. He can get fussy, concerned and fearful over the weather and deprive himself of the comfort and security radar is designed to give. But how much better to reckon on this fantastic device, sit back, relax, and enjoy the trip.

God does not promise immunity from trouble, but He does promise to make us "more than conquerors." He does not guarantee good weather, but He does guarantee to take a man through it.

In fact, the man who is led by God discovers that He is able to turn trouble into blessing, tragedy into triumph.

You may choose to fly "blind" into the future, or you can choose to allow God to guide you. You may choose to live as though He doesn't care or isn't able to help you, or you may take Him at His word and enjoy the safety and security He delights to give. "If God be for us, who can be against us? —Romans 8:31.

❖❖❖❖❖❖❖❖❖❖❖

What qualifies the "All things" of verse 28? Why is there no possibility of condemnation or judgment for the one who trusts in Christ?

Christian View Of History

Romans 8:18-25

History doesn't make sense if you look for meaning inside it. A man will never completely understand the world situation as it is (in fact he'll never understand himself) until he sees behind the scenes an irreconcilable conflict between two kingdoms, the kingdom of good and the kingdom of evil, the kingdom of God and the kingdom of Satan. History is meaningless—"a tale told by an idiot, full of sound and fury, signifying nothing"—unless seen in the light of this fundamental conflict between righteousness and wickedness.

Back of the tension in the world, underneath the conflict, the pressures and strife, is this inexorable ambition of Satan in his deceptive, insidious strategy to win the world. This spiritual warfare breaks out here and there into physical wars: personal, domestic, industrial, civil or international. But these wars are the symptoms of a great unseen warfare.

A warfare in which the ultimate triumph of Christ is absolutely certain.

History makes sense, civilization makes sense, a man's personal life makes sense only in terms of a plan outside history. Imagine a line one thousand miles long (or a hundred thousand, it makes no difference for it is infinite). Let this line represent eternity. Now imagine a space six inches long marked off on that line. Those six inches represent time from beginning to end. Let a pin point on those six inches represent our present civilization within that history. Look for meaning within that pinpoint, within that six inches, you get the idea. *History makes sense only in terms of eternity.*

Imagine a second line representing a divine purpose. It begins at the begining of the thousand-mile line and continues to the end of it. That purpose moves right through the six inches of history, right through the pin point of our civilization. And that divine purpose gives meaning to the six inches of history and the pin point of our civilization.

God is at work in history. He is beyond history, but He has a purpose which is being worked out through history. It is this purpose of God's that causes history to make sense. It is God's purpose for life to make sense! In fact, the idea of progress did not exist before the Old Testament. It is from the Bible that the concept of progress comes. As it has been put, "History is His Story." "For God has allowed us to know the secret of His plan, and it is this; He purposes in His sovereign will that all human history shall be consummated in Jesus Christ, that everything that exists in heaven or in earth shall find its perfection and its fulfillment in Him." —Ephesians 1:9-10.[1]

❊❊❊❊❊❊❊❊❊❊❊❊

If you have a copy of J. B. Phillip's version of the New Testament Epistles, read Romans 8:18-25 from that version. There is no other passage of scripture, or for that matter, no piece of literature, which sets forth such a comprehensive over-view of history in such a brief compass. Here Paul declares the "futility" which we feel today, the restlessness of all creation to be emancipated from the "tyranny of change and decay." Collective man is restless, like a woman in childbirth. The labor pains are closer together and they are increasing in intensity. This says Paul, is to be expected. We have a hope, which hope is fulfilled in the return of Jesus Christ. *All that the entire created universe seeks for will come in Christ!*

---

[1] J. B. Phillips, *The New Testament In Modern English* (New York: Macmillan Company, 1958)

Jesus Christ In The Old Testament

Christian faith is rooted and grounded in history! Its strength is its foundation in fact. It is encouraging to the Christian businessman, fighting the economic battle in uncertain days, to realize that what he does on his job today has some connection with what God is doing in history. There is a continuity between now and eternity, and his job today is involved in that continuity.

A philosophy of life is important to the "hard-nosed" businessman. Whether he realizes it or not, his day-to-day actions are based upon some sort of an overview of life, even though he may not have spelled it out in so many words. His point of view, his goals are fundamental to his job, and nothing elevates a man's sights and sharpens his activity like the sense of being God's man, right where he is, day in, day out. Getting the connection between the Old and New Testaments as it relates to Jesus

Christ is not meant to be simply intellectual exercise, but a practical lesson to help the busy man get this sense of God's activity in history.

Furthermore, contrary to the rather common assumption that historical Judaism and Christianity are in opposition, it is good to know that they are two halves of one whole. Christianity flows from Judaism and the continuity is significant and helpful. Neither can be fully understood without the other.

One more thing. The Old Testament was written over a period of 1500 years by many authors, living in entirely different times and cultures. The last book in the Old Testament is nearly 500 years earlier than the first book in the New Testament. There is no greater verification of the validity of the Old and New Testaments than fulfilled prophecy, and no prophecy was more important than that concerning Jesus. Literally hundreds of specific details in His life were predicted hundreds of years before they occurred, a fact which testifies to the supernatural source of the Bible. It had many writers, but one Author. "Search the Scriptures (when John was writing, the only Scriptures would have been the Old Testament), for in them ye think ye have eternal life; and they are they which testify of me."—John 5:39.

JESUS CHRIST IN THE OLD TESTAMENT

For an interesting and spiritually nourishing experience, make a comparative study of the following Scriptures from the Old and New Testament. Use a paper and pencil as you discover the things predicted and the events fulfilled. Compare Isaiah 7:14 with Matthew 1:18-25 and Luke 1:26-38; Micah 5:2 with Luke 2:1-20; Deuteronomy 18:15, 18-19 with Acts 3:22-26; Zechariah 9:9 with Matthew 21:1-9; Isaiah 53:3 with John 1:11, 12:37-43; Isaiah 53:7 with Matthew 27:12-14, Mark 15:3-4, and Luke 23:8-10; Isaiah 50:6 with Matthew 26:27; 27:30, Mark 14:65, 15:9 and Luke 22:63-64; Psalm 22:7-8 with Matthew 27:39-43; Isaiah 53:5-6 with John 1:29, 1 Corinthians 15:3 and 1 Peter 2:24-25; Psalm 22:14-16 with John 19:15-18; Isaiah 53:12 with Luke 23:32-34; Psalm 22:18 with John 19:23-24; Psalm 16:10 with 1 Corinthians 15:4 8, Romans 4:25 and Acts 2:22-32.

The Way To Begin
The New Year

Philippians 3:8-15

There's something irresistible about New Year's resolutions—even to the most sophisticated. He may
not discuss it, but a man usually finds a peculiar satisfaction in the close of an old year, the birth of the
new. Things are going to be different, he's going to
make some changes . . . even if he doesn't share this
determination with others for fear he may fail
to follow through and suffer humiliation before
them.

January 1 has strong appeal and the perceptive
man isn't going to let the golden hour of a new start
escape without some personal inventory—some decision regarding the future.

As in all the basics of life, Christian faith is relevant here. Christ's way is THE way to capitalize on
beginnings. In fact, it is the only practical way!
Only in Christ can a man really be new . . . and only
in Christ does this newness persevere. Renewal is

continual for the man in Christ. *Man in Christ is man at his best.*

The Apostle was an old man when he wrote Philippians, and he had suffered much for Christ, but he had vision like a youngster, and his vision is reflected in this passage in Philippians. "That I may know Him and the power of His resurrection, and may share in His sufferings . . ." (Verse 10) ". . . forgetting what lies behind and straining forward to what lies ahead, I press on toward the goal . . ."—Philippians 3:13, 14. (R.S.V.)

❖❖❖❖❖❖❖❖❖❖❖

Try to put the Apostle's goal into your own words. What impresses you most about this purpose?

The Reasonable Remedy

But what does a man do about past failure and sin? Here's where moral reformation invariably breaks down. Someone has described guilt as "perhaps the most corrosive emotion the human spirit has to bear." The guilty past pesters a man, haunts his resolutions, dulls his determination. Like a malignant infection, guilt gnaws away at his vitality. Guilt is a malicious accuser that dogs a man, shames him, discourages him, sucks initiative and drive out of resolution. What's the remedy for the demoralizing impact of guilt?

With sweet reasonableness, God Himself, speaking through His prophet, asks man to consider what He is ready to do for him. The blackest sin can be purged and cleansed—and forgotten, if a man will only come to the Lord for the aid He stands ready to give.

Significantly, the new man in Christ is always

working on a clean sheet. Each moment represents fresh opportunity by virtue of the forgiveness of God in Christ and the perpetual renewal of Divine grace.

"If we walk in the light as He is in the light, we have fellowship with one another and the blood of Jesus Christ God's son, keeps on cleansing us from all sin."—1 John 1:7.

❖❖❖❖❖❖❖❖❖❖❖

How does a man get rid of guilt? Mark the fact that the prophet invites to "reason" together. *The Christian solution to sin is not irrational.* It is the man who refuses to consider who is unreasonable.

The Original Sin

Genesis 3:1-12

"Where art thou?" The first question God addressed to man. God knew—but He could not help Adam until he answered. God asked to give man the opportunity to be honest about himself and tell God where he was.

It is a familiar question: You lose your way, phone ahead for directions, the first question asked you is, "Where are you?" He must know where you are before he can direct you to your destination. Where you are has a great deal to do with where you are going!

Adam was hiding from God—hiding for fear of God—hiding behind excuses (Genesis 3:12-13). How human it is to make excuses instead of admitting sin. God, in His infinite patience, waits for each of us, waits until we tell Him where we are. He knows . . . but we must come out of hiding before

He can forgive and renew us. God can't love a man if he won't let Him!

The man who is lost will never make his destination until he faces himself honestly, admits his lostness, tells God where he is.

"For the first time in eighteen years, I quit blaming my wife, my mother-in-law and my boss for the mess that was me," said a former alcoholic. He came out of hiding, admitted his need, and God began to work in his life.

Where are YOU?

The blood of Christ cannot cleanse excuses, it only cleanses sin. "If we confess our sins, He is faithful and just to forgive us our sins, and to cleanse us from all unrighteousness."—1 John 1:9.

❖❖❖❖❖❖❖❖❖❖❖

Without trying to be theological, what was the real temptation Eve faced? What was the result of her surrender? What sin is involved in this situation?

Your Life, A Plan Of God

Ephesians 1:3-10

Does God have a plan for each man? If so, how does he discover it? How can one know God's will?

A superficial reading of the Bible reveals that the men of the Bible were led by God. Their leadership flowed from their obedience to God's will. They were able to lead others because they were led by God. Jesus Christ Himself is the pre-eminent example of a God-planned life. He taught many things by precept and parable, but the supreme lesson of His life was its absolute conformity to His Father's will.

Man was made to be God-led, and he falls short of manhood unless and until he is. Only God knows all the built-in possibilities of a man, and only He can direct so that every ability with which a man is endowed at birth is given full expression in life. The man who is led by God realizes the maximum utilization of his potential. *As a man fulfills God's will, he fulfills himself!*

YOUR LIFE, A PLAN OF GOD

"For God has allowed us to know the secret of His plan and it is this: He purposes in His sovereign will that all human history shall be consummated in Christ; that everything that exists in heaven or in earth shall find its perfection and fulfillment in Him."—Ephesians 1:9-10[1].

❖❖❖❖❖❖❖❖❖❖❖

Pay special attention to the verbs in this passage of Scripture. What tense are they? To whom do they refer? What meaning does this have for you?

[1] J. B. Phillips, *The New Testament In Modern English* (New York: Macmillan Company, 1958)

The Inerrant
Guidance Of God

Here is one of the most beautiful and practical incidents in the Bible demonstrating how the will of God is understood. The key to the passage is verse 27. Note the simplicity of the arrangement.

Knowing God's will is NOT complicated. "I being in the way, the Lord led me." The servant was "in the way," therefore, "the Lord led."

Man's side is to be "in the way." God's side is "to lead." Do not confuse these. They are the two orientation points in knowing and doing God's will. God promises to lead the man who puts himself in the way to be led. Man does not have the responsibility to figure out God's will, this is God's part. Man's part is to be "in the way." Man's part is to be available.

However He does it, God will make known His way to the man who waits to walk in it. This is not an over-simplification. Count on God to lead, never mind how. He promises so to do! Be sure you are committed to His will, ready to be led, then depend upon Him to keep His side of the bargain. Whether or not you feel you are being led is immaterial. You have God's promise. Count on it! "I being in the way, the Lord led me."—Genesis 24:27.

❋❋❋❋❋❋❋❋❋❋❋

Notice that in the case of Abraham's servant, confidence came when it was all over. He undoubtedly suffered some qualms in the process, but he persevered, putting his confidence in God to overrule his error or misjudgment. The correct outcome did not depend on the servant's judgment, but upon God's faithfulness.

Your Way Can Be Sure

Proverbs 3:5-10

Remember there are two orientation points in this matter of being God-led, God's side and man's side. Man's is to be "in the way." God's is to lead.

In this passage, man's side is expressed in three conditions, God's side in a promise. (1) "Trust in the Lord with all thine heart . . . . ." Trust is defined as "unquestioning resting in its object." *Trust the Lord,* not your own feelings, your own wisdom, or your experience. *Trust the Lord,* relax, never question His integrity.

(2) ". . . lean not unto thine own understanding." This is the negative statement of the same principle. This does not say, "do not reason." God puts no premium on ignorance . . . but He does say you should not put the weight of decision down upon your own understanding. Put the weight upon God.

(3) ". . . in all thy ways acknowledge Him. . ." That is, recognize God in everything. To quote Paul,

"Whether you eat or drink or whatever you do, do all to the glory of God." Let God into everything, hide nothing from Him. Meet these three conditions and "He shall direct thy paths." No doubt here! You meet the simple conditions, then reckon implicitly on God's faithfulness.

❖❖❖❖❖❖❖❖❖❖❖

Is it possible for a man to be rational and yet not "lean unto his own understanding?" Think through the full connotation of the word "trust." What does it mean to you?

The Committed Life

Psalm 37:5

Here again are clearly suggested the two sides to the matter of Divine guidance. The Psalmist suggests two conditions and a promise which accrues when the conditions are met. The two conditions are incumbent upon man, and when met, God fulfills His promise.

(1) "Commit . . . " A word suggesting "rolling off one's burden on another." As one commits a legal matter to an attorney, or a medical matter to a physician, so he commits his way to the Lord. He chooses to allow the Lord to "take over" in his life. He gets himself off his own hands into the Lord's. He decides to let God direct his affairs.

(2) "Trust . . ." The Lord Himself is the object of trust, not a man's feelings or his understanding. Trust Him, His integrity, His word. Meet these two conditions, invites the Psalmist, and God *guarantees* to "bring it to pass" or work it out.

We need to remember again and again that it is really God who works these things out. It isn't simply that He helps us a little bit, He actually does the working out. When a man lets God into a situation, God goes to work in that situation and all the resources of God are brought to bear upon it. *All God seeks is man's invitation to take over.*

How God Leads

Proverbs 16:3

God may use many different methods to lead a man right. The important thing is to realize that He leads!

God may engineer circumstances so a man has no alternatives and there is only one way to go.

He may "speak" through a passage of Scripture or through the word of a friend or a sermon.

But the final test is inward—what might be called intuition. This may be thought of as the "still small voice" within. Assuming a man's openness to the will of God, his intuition can be trusted. "Commit thy works unto the Lord . . . and *thy thoughts shall be established.*"

Paul speaks of having "the mind of Christ." Whatever other means God may use to guide, He will establish a man's thoughts. God's Spirit within checks or releases a man one way or another. ("Where the Spirit of the Lord is, there is liberty.") The man who is seeking to know and do God's will may trust the gentle inner restraint of the Spirit. However, it is important to note that spiritual intuition will never be contrary to the will of God as revealed in the Bible. God is consistent with His word and in all matters of faith and life, the Bible is the final authority. The Spirit never leads contrary to it!—2 Timothy 3:16-17.

❖❖❖❖❖❖❖❖❖❖❖❖❖

Think through this matter of decision. What are the characteristics of a decisive person? Does he come to his decisions entirely through reason, or is another element involved? What makes one man able to make decisions more quickly and accurately than another? Is it just superior logic, or something more.

Man's Reasonable Service

Romans 12:1-2

✦✦✦✦✦✦✦✦✦✦✦✦

These two verses are the summation of the whole matter of knowing and doing God's will. Here, as in the Psalms, the author states the conditions for being led and makes it clear that a man may "prove" God's will by meeting these conditions. The word prove means to "test by experience." Hence one who "presents his body a living sacrifice" and is "not conformed to this world but transformed by the renewing of his mind," will see the will of God being worked out in his day to day affairs.

The test as to whether or not God's will is being done is not how the man feels about it, but whether or not he has met the conditions. God certainly will not fall back on His word, therefore if the conditions are being met, one may safely assume that what comes next in his life is the will of God. Having kept his part of the bargain, a man entertains no doubt whatever as to God's honoring of His promise.

❖❖❖❖❖❖❖❖❖❖❖❖

"How can I know that God is leading me?" is a normal question. The answer lies not in a man's "feeling led" or any other emotion. Feelings are fickle and deceptive. God's promise is true and irrevocable. I am sure of God's will because I did what He instructed me to do and I am absolutely sure that He will therefore do what He said He would.

CHAPTER

THREE

Man Of Conviction

The Peril Of Tolerance

1 John 4:1-6

Tolerance may mean simply Godless indifference. A man will tolerate everything if he is without conviction. Believing nothing, he will fall for anything. Of course there is a brand of intolerance that is nothing more than blind bigotry. Rather than think, a man may battle all who disagree with Him. He thinks he is thinking when actually he is only rearranging his prejudices. Rigid, inflexible intolerance, or soft, flabby tolerance are equally wrong.

On the other hand, intolerance is the hallmark of truth and integrity. The reliable pharmacist is intolerant of incorrect prescriptions or carelessness in their preparation. The physicist is intolerant of error in his equations. The engineer is intolerant of sub-standard materials. There is no compromise with poison, no intelligent way to appease error. Sentimental tolerance in a man or a nation is the precursor to ruin.

Nineteen hundred years ago Rome and Greece had reached the apex of their civilization. Rome had built the greatest empire, Greece had developed the finest language and philosophy. Both were completely tolerant of any and all religion. Rome accommodated any god, because it kept peace within her borders. Greece built alters to all the gods, even one to "an unknown god." And those days of unprecedented toleration were days of unprecedented depravity and corruption, the culture of Rome and Greece notwithstanding. The floors of the amphitheaters ran red with blood of the slain. The man who could invent a more brutal way of destroying life was hailed as a public hero. Cultured, intelligent, sophisticated, tolerant people ringed the amphitheater, lusting for blood, howling like a pack of wolves for the death blow by their favorite gladiator. They were totally tolerant and totally Godless and totally depraved!

Godly intolerance, not prejudice, is the backbone of a strong, healthy civilization. It is incumbent upon each man to examine his own heart as to whether or not he is tolerant simply because he doesn't care!

"Woe to you, scribes and Pharisees, hypocrites! For you build the tombs of the prophets and adorn the monuments of the righteous, saying 'If we had lived in the days of our fathers, we would not have taken part with them in shedding the blood of the prophets.' Thus you witness against yourselves, that you are sons of those who murdered the prophets. Fill up, then, the measure of your fathers. You serpents, you brood of vipers, how are you to escape being sentenced to hell?"—Jesus in Matthew 23:29-33. (R.S.V.)

❖❖❖❖❖❖❖❖❖❖❖❖

Notice that the Apostle John commands Christians not to believe all teachers. This is not optional with believers, they are to be selective, to discern between truth and error, to accept truth and repudiate error. It is interesting to observe that this admonition concerning the critical examination of teachers precedes some of John's most penetrating words on love. Intolerance and love are not incompatible.

No Man Is Without A God

Acts 17:22-31

Every man has a god.

Even the atheist! He believes in No-god and is often more zealous, more religious about his belief in No-god than some men who believe in God. It is not easy to have faith in No-god. Such a faith is held against overwhelming evidence to the contrary. In fact, the only thing that "saves face" for the atheist is the fact of God's existence. Nobody would take an athiest seriously if there were no God. Anymore than they would take seriously a man who made a big deal out of proving there is no Santa Claus. Why pay attention to a man who labors to disprove what is non-existent?

God is, therefore the athiest is not shadow boxing or beating the air. He's conducting a real war against a real Opponent. The fact of God's existence is what gives the athiest status.

The real question is not whether or not a man

believes in God, but what kind of a God does he serve? One man serves the god Mammon. Money is everything! The whole energy of his life is thrown into the acquisition of Wealth. The more he gets, the more he wants! Enough is never! Mammon is a hard taskmaster, a merciless tyrant. It has destroyed many.

Another puts Pleasure first, follows a giddy, shallow, senseless round of froth. He takes Pleasure wherever he finds it, hungrily devours it like a starved animal tearing at a cadaver. The tragedy is that it takes more and more Pleasure to get less and less satisfaction. The point of diminishing returns is reached quickly. Genuine delight decreases in inverse ratio to increased effort. The pitiful pay-off is a hollow life, emptiness, a bubble.

Still another serves the god Fame or Power or Prestige, or the worst tyrant of all, the god Self, and inevitably reaps what he sows. The thing is, man becomes like his god. *He grows into the image of that which he worships.*

"This is life eternal, to know thee, the only true God, and Jesus Christ whom thou hast sent."—John 17:3.

✦✦✦✦✦✦✦✦✦✦✦

The Greeks were so incurably religious that they had an altar to every conceivable god, even to "an unknown god." Their real problem is mentioned in

Acts 17:21. They were utterly academic about everything. They were not particularly interested in embracing truth, simply to hear it. Their counterpart on the contemporary scene is the man who always has an "open mind." He forgets that an open mind never closes on the truth it receives. Truth just goes in and out without ever lodging there. Such men are "tolerant" for the simple reason that they have nothing to be intolerant about. Nothing, that is, except their intolerance of the man with real conviction.

You Can Prove It To Your Own Satisfaction

John 20:24-31

The most fascinating personality ever to stride into history was the man called Jesus. His teaching is considered to be the greatest, His life unimpeachable, having personified every known virtue. The claims He made for Himself confounded His generation and have mystified and challenged every generation since. He suffered the ignominy of death by crucifixion as a common criminal. His life is the focal center of time—the "hinge of history," dividing it into B. C. and A. D. The Encyclopedia Britannica gives 20,000 words to His life. Surely that man is uninformed, whatever he knows, who is unfamiliar with Jesus Christ!

Men have had many doubts concerning Jesus through the centuries, but no generation has doubted Him more than His own. The majority frankly refused the evidence and rejected Him. Others, though they could not understand Him, with honest objectivity accepted the abundant evidence and were led to remarkable devotion to Jesus.

Two things are significant in the passage under consideration: First, Thomas, one of the disciples, seriously doubted and Jesus met this doubt with acceptable proof. Second, the author of the fourth Gospel frankly states the purpose of his writing (20:31). He presents the evidence that men might be led to faith in Jesus Christ and thus to the experience of eternal life. Jesus said, "if any man's will is to do His will, he shall know whether the teaching is from God or whether I am speaking on my own authority."—John 7:17. (R.S.V.)

✤✤✤✤✤✤✤✤✤✤✤✤

Jesus asks no man to accept Him on "blind faith." In fact there is no such thing as blind faith. There can be no faith where there is not first knowledge. Faith implies an object in which to rest. John's Gospel is like a lab manual which contains certain data for personal experimentation regarding Jesus. Certain conditions are laid down which if met, will lead to certain results. These results are predictable. Compare John 20:31 with 1:12-13 or 3:16 or 5:24. Note 1 John 5:11-12 in this context. Observe in John 7:17 that Jesus says willingness to obey is the condition to be shown. Willingness to be shown is the first prerequisite for the so-called "scientific method."

The Three-In-One God

John 1:1-14

Jesus Christ did not begin when He was born in Bethlehem! He had always existed. There never was a time when He was not.

His manhood began when He was born of a virgin, but He had always existed as the Son of God. Incidentally, the term Son of God does not signify one who is somehow less than God. Son of God is an eternal designation. The more familiar one becomes with the Bible, the more clearly does he see that God is presented as a Being Who is eternally the Father, the Son and the Holy Spirit. The Son and the Spirit are not inferior to the Father, although they are subordinate to Him. This subordination is one of administration, not of substance or essence. Functionally the Son is obedient to the Father and the Spirit is obedient to the Father and the Son. The theological word for this is "Trinity."

The word "Trinity" is not found in the Bible,

but the fact which this word is intended to describe does! Three Persons are revealed in the Bible as co-equal and co-eternal. They are the Father, the Son, the Holy Spirit. Deity is attributed to each of them. They are not each one-third of a whole God, they are each fully God. Yet the Bible does not present three Gods, but One, and He, a three-in-one God. "Godhead" is the English translation of the Greek word used to describe this unique fact of eternity. Simply because one cannot understand this is no reason for rejecting it. Efforts to reconcile the three-in-one aspect of the Godhead only succeed in explaining away either the Deity of the Son and the Spirit, or the unity of the Godhead. Both are true, and because God is God, man cannot fully comprehend infinity.

Jesus said, "I and Father are one . . . he that hath seen Me hath seen the Father."

****

Verse 14 of John 1 is one of the key verses of the Bible. God's method of self-disclosure is "truth through personality." God makes Himself known by becoming man. This is the meaning of "incarnation," God clothed in human flesh. Why do you think John refers to Jesus as "The Word?"

Behold Sin's Remedy

John 1:19-34

The birth of Jesus was miraculous, the only one of its kind in history, prophesied by Isaiah seven hundred years before it happened (Isaiah 7:14) as being the supreme historical evidence of God's personal visitation among men. But in a sense John the Baptist's introduction of Jesus was even more startling. "Behold the Lamb of God . . ." He might have presented Jesus as "The Lion of the Tribe of Judah," or "The Prince of Peace," or "Emanuel" which means "God with us," but no, he chose to introduce Him as "the Lamb of God."

There was nothing vague or ambiguous about this title to those who heard. "Lamb of God" meant one thing to the Jews, it meant sacrifice. From the days of father Abraham, "Lamb of God" signified atonement for sin. John chose to present Jesus with the title which told of His purpose in coming. He came as a sacrifice for sin, and Jesus will never be understood by those who are unable to see Him first as the Saviour. Everything Jesus said about Himself was either to qualify Himself as the Saviour of men or to show forth by what means He would be the Saviour.

Thus did John the Baptist, the second "Elijah," who was to precede and announce the "debut" of God's Son to the world He had come to save, introduce Him: "Behold the Lamb of God that taketh away the sin of the world."—John 1:29. Thus did Jesus begin His remarkable, albeit brief three-year ministry among the world of men.

❖❖❖❖❖❖❖❖❖❖❖

How do you explain the fact that so many simply refused to accept the death of Jesus Christ on the cross as a sacrificial substitute for man's sin? This teaching is inescapable in the Bible. To remove all references to His death and every record of His death from the New Testament would leave very little of the New Testament. His death by crucifixion as a sacrifice for sin is inextricably intertwined with all He said and did, all the Apostles said and did.

Jesus And Himself

John 2:12-22

Consider the SELF-CONSCIOUSNESS of Jesus. No study you make will yield more spiritual profit than to examine the Scriptures from the point of view of Jesus' self-awareness. You will find it interesting, informative, challenging and exceedingly nourishing. Help yourself to some of the meat of the Word.

What did Jesus think of Himself? What was He aware of concerning His life, His purpose, His nature, His destiny? Some have attempted to show that the entire supernatural aspect of Jesus was a product of man's fabrication. To put it in the words of one very secular person, "Jesus just had some of the best public relations men in the business." Some theologians have said the same thing in finer language. They have declared that the Jesus of the Gospels and the Christ of Paul's epistles are completely different. They accuse Paul of inventing a

supernatural being called Christ who is totally unlike the man called Jesus in the Gospel record.

Honest reading of the New Testament will show
quite plainly that Jesus Christ was not, nor could
He have been, the product of a Madison Avenue
gimmick or a theological invention of Paul, the
Apostle. See for yourself!

The fact of Jesus is indisputable! He actually lived
in a certain place at a certain time in history. He
thought certain things and felt certain things about
Himself, and happily, He revealed many of His
thoughts and feelings by His remarks. The record
includes an abundance of information which dis-
closes the self-consciousness of Jesus.

It is important to realize that the record stands
on its own two feet, so to speak. The historicity,
accuracy and authenticity of the Gospel accounts
are no longer seriously disputed. Furthermore, one
has only to read them for himself to know that the
facts are humanly uninventable. No man, not the
greatest literary genius who ever lived, could think
up the claims Jesus made for Himself. They are
utterly unlike the statements made by characters
in fiction. They are literally "out of this world."
Yet there is a simplicity, a naturalness, an unimag-
inativeness about them which bespeaks their realism.
Jesus must have thought these things, said these

things about Himself—no man could have fabricated them, least of all the writers of the Gospels. These sayings of Jesus are obviously the record of an eye witness who is reporting simply and directly what he saw and heard. "For the life was manifested, and we have seen it, and bear witness . . . "—1 John 1:2.

✽✽✽✽✽✽✽✽✽✽✽✽

Bearing in mind that Luke was a man of science, a medical doctor, trained after the finest tradition (Hippocratic) of Medical Science, the process of diagnosis by careful, controlled observation, examine the opening verses of Luke's Gospel. (Luke 1:1-4) Everything Dr. Luke reports is in agreement and harmony with that which Matthew, Mark, John and the Apostle Paul record.

Lord Of The Sabbath

John 5:19-47

Jesus had healed a man ill for 38 years. But the healing took place on the Sabbath and this aroused the wrath of the Pharisees, the strictest sect of Judaism, and they began to persecute Jesus. The fact that a helpless invalid had been restored to health and strength was immaterial. Actually, the fact that it had been done on the Sabbath was immaterial also. These Pharisees were determined to dispose of Jesus in one way or another and they would use any means, fair or foul, to do it.

But their justification for persecuting Jesus was the transgression of their religious law. Again and again Jesus pointed out to the Pharisees how by clever rationalizing they had managed to break their Sabbath whenever it suited their need. They were the masters of religious trivia and much of this trivia was devised to help them keep the letter of the law even though they transgressed its spirit. Now a man, totally incapacitated for 38 years, is healed by Jesus on the Sabbath and the Pharisees sought to kill Jesus. Incredible—but those are the facts! Their righteous indignation was exceeded only by their unspeakable hypocrisy.

However, as a result of the discussion which followed, Jesus boldly claimed a unique relationship with almighty God which is absolutely ludicrous if untrue. The fanatical religionists of His day were never able to intimidate Jesus. Every effort they made to discredit Him ended in an expose of their own infamous bigotry and deceit. The point here is that Jesus confronts men who are determined to liquidate Him with claims that are astounding to say the least. These claims had to be true or Jesus would have long since been relegated to the category of unacceptable fairy tales. "He who does not honor the Son does not honor the Father Who sent Him." —John 5:23. (R.S.V.)

❖❖❖❖❖❖❖❖❖❖❖❖

Notice especially the words in verses 17 and 18, 19-23, 25-27, 36-38, 46 and 47. Put any of these claims on the lips of any other great man in history, what would be the public reaction to him had he made these claims for himself? Either Jesus was what He claimed, or He was the greatest fraud ever foisted on humanity, or He was a psychotic. No normal person would make such claims unless they were true!

Never Hunger —
Never Thirst

Following the very familiar incident in which Jesus quieted the stormy sea (verses 16-21), the crowds missed Him, and went to Capernaum to find Him. His dissertation on the bread of life resulted. This is one of the most beautiful passages in the Gospels. It is one of the most difficult to understand also. In fact, so difficult is it, that many disciples are offended by it, and refuse to "go along" with Jesus anymore (See verse 66).

Jesus begins this message with a mild rebuke against the materialistic incentive that brought the crowd (verse 26), followed by one of the most interesting admonitions of His ministry. "Labor for the food . . . which the Son of Man will give you. . ." (verse 27) How does a man labor for that which is given? Fortunately the answer is given in the context, verse 29. One cannot overestimate the significance of this answer. Men who think of religion as primarily a matter of works should ponder long and hard such a statement as found in John 6:29.

Can you imagine Abraham Lincoln, for example, making such a statement as is found in verse 35? Of course the first answer to such a question is that he didn't—and wouldn't. But suppose he had, and suppose he had expected men to take him seriously when he said it (Jesus did), what would his contemporaries have thought of him? You see, the statements of Jesus about Himself just do not fit any other personality, however eminent, yet they fit Jesus. Somehow one is not suprised to hear Him say these things. He doesn't seem to be "out of character" at such times. There is a fundamental unity and continuity between His character, His conduct, and His claims.

While considering the unprecedented nature of the statement in verse 35, do not overlook the phenomenal nature of the proposition. *The man who takes Jesus seriously in this, finds a never-ending provision for the deepest needs of his life.* "Never hunger . . . never thirst." Tremendous! Think of it! Midst all the empty, unsatisfying experiences of life, the foods that never nourish, the wells that run dry, the roads that lead to dead ends, the illusive promises that never pay off, Jesus promises ENOUGH indefinitely!

Not only satisfaction from the standpoint of provision is offered here, but from the standpoint of security also. You'll never find four verses (37-40) in the Bible more packed full of God's promise of absolute security for time and eternity. Look also at verses 44-47.

No wonder Peter said, "Lord, to whom shall we go? You have the words of eternal life!"—John 6:68. (R.S.V.)

❊❊❊❊❊❊❊❊❊❊❊

Difficult as this passage is, it will yield rich treasure to the man who digs into it. Here's a good place to practice some "depth study." Take plenty of time to read slowly and think carefully through these tremendous verses. Examine the unusual claim in verses 50 and 51. You also see the kind of rationalizing the unbeliever resorts to when confronted with the truth he is not willing to accept (verses 41-42).

Jesus: Egomaniac,
Or Truth

John 8:12-30

Jesus Christ is known to be the most humble Man Who ever lived. He represented humility at its apex. He was humility personified, yet He used the personal pronoun "I" as much as, or more than any other public figure—at least anyone who has made any sort of a contribution whatsoever to civilization. Jesus and humility are virtually synonymous in the minds of men. How then do you reconcile this paradoxical egocentricity? How is it possible for Him to make these astounding claims for Himself and yet never have His sincerity, or His humility . . . or His sanity doubted? Actually, what Jesus says about Himself is becoming to Him. It does not seem unusual or incongruous for Him to say these incredible things about Himself.

One of the reasons men take Jesus so matter-of-factly is they don't really THINK about Him. So few men read the New Testament intelligently. You ought to read the New Testament like you read the newspaper, to get the story. Or like you read the financial page, to get the facts. Trouble is, we are so inclined to read-into the narrative things we already know, and we miss the fresh information that ought to make us "sit up and take notice" occasionally. Try reading this passage in John as though you had never heard of Jesus before, or at least had not made up your mind about Him. Read it as though you wanted to know exactly what He said and what He meant by what He said. Read it to get the facts.

When read with this kind of objectivity, some of the things Jesus says in this passage are really staggering. They really jar a man! Take for example His word in verse 23. Or the remarkable statement of verse 24. Think these through and you're driven to dismiss Jesus as a fake or an egomaniac—or you may do as some have, discredit the record itself as unreliable . . . or worship Jesus as God—or reject Him, knowing you are turning your back on Truth. Jesus said, "Even if I do bear witness to myself, my testimony is true, for I know whence I have come and whither I am going . . ."—John 8:14. (R.S.V.)

❉❉❉❉❉❉❉❉❉❉❉❉

On the basis of verse 19, what are the alternatives so far as belief in God is concerned, if one rejects

Jesus? What do you guess to be the import of the question put to Jesus by the Pharisees in verse 19? Where did Jesus say He came from? Taken at face value, the claim Jesus makes in verse 29 is really amazing. Is Jesus boasting, or merely stating a fact?

Jesus Is Jehovah ("I Am")

John 8:31-59

No wonder they took up stones to throw at Him. They had a law concerning blasphemy, and by their law the blasphemer should be stoned until dead. In the plain light of the New Testament it is impossible to understand that person who insists that Jesus never claimed equality with God. How anyone can read the New Testament with any perception whatever and come up with an idea so contrary to the fact is a mystery. Over and over in His almost continual conflict with the Pharisees during His public ministry, His claim to deity was the issue. Or look at it this way, the Pharisees accused Him of blasphemy, of making Himself equal with God, and Jesus never once attempted to dispossess them of this accusation. Not once did Jesus try to make the Pharisees see that they had misunderstood Him when they thought He was claiming equality with God. He allowed their indictment to stand, and what's more, He usually countered their accusation with language which caused the religionists to gnash their teeth in righteous horror.

This incident recorded in John is a case in point. The Jews had tried earlier to provoke some discussion concerning Jesus' father, (verse 19) but Jesus overlooked it at the moment. Now, however, they come to the point of their earlier insinuation and without any subtlety accuse Him of being illegitimate. Ignoring this reference to His virgin birth, Jesus confounds His opposition by declaring that He antedated Abraham, the first Hebrew. This was bad enough, but in so doing Jesus referred to Himself using the most sacred name of God in the Jewish Bible. "Before Abraham was, I AM." The devout Jew would not even pronounce this holy name of God, "I AM." So they took up stones to stone Him. If Jesus wasn't equal with God, He let the Jews believe He thought He was! (Look up John 10: 31-33)

There are two or three things in this particular exchange between Jesus and the religious opposition which are significant. In a day when there is so much talk about tolerance, a day in which the man who holds a conviction with any certainty is in danger of being called a bigot, it is refreshing to see the candid way in which Jesus handled the hypocrisy of the Pharisees. One instance of this is seen by putting verses 38 and 44 together. There are times when tolerance is not a virtue, but weakness. There is certainly no virtue in being tolerant if one holds no convictions, and it is not uncommon for the man who believes nothing, who speaks the most of tolerance, to be the most intolerant of one who really believes something. Jesus' absolute intolerance of sin and error was in no way inconsistent with His love for men, even the sinner or the liar.

The simple logic of Jesus in this passage is also very interesting. Notice verses 45, 47 and 55. Jesus cannot deny Himself. One can almost feel His compassion show through here. In spite of their hypocrisy and blind unbelief, He tries to reason with them. But they were simply incapable of being reasonable. This is the way of unbelief. "Why do you not understand what I say?"—John 8:43. (R.S.V.)

❈❈❈❈❈❈❈❈❈❈❈

In the light of this discussion about Jesus' relation to Abraham and His pre-existence before Abraham, you will find it interesting to compare John 8:58 with Exodus 3:13-14. With reference to verse 41, at least the Pharisees were consistent, either Jesus was born of a virgin or He was born out of wedlock.

He Could Not Be Killed

These amazing claims Jesus made for Himself! How did He get away with it? It is unrealistic to say that these claims were not made by Him, that they were interpolated into the text of the narrative sometime subsequent to its origin by misguided disciples. Take the claims out of the narrative and there's nothing left. It would be impossible to piece together any semblance of a narrative with any continuity if one should delete the things Jesus said about Himself. In most cases the events of His life are inseparably joined to the things He said.

Jesus made these claims because they were true, and His enemies found it impossible to discredit Him because His life was absolutely consistent with the claims. His sincerity, His integrity, His naturalness, His realism, His simplicity were undeniable. This was what drove the opposition to irrational extremes. They were beside themselves with rage because every encounter with Jesus left them more vulnerable, more obvious, more exposed, more disillusioned in themselves. Every question designed to catch Jesus was turned back upon the questioner leaving him speechless and humiliated.

Here again Jesus uses the personal pronoun "I." Here again He speaks of Himself in a role only Deity can fill. This passage is most comforting to the one who trusts Jesus Christ. Jesus is the "Good Shepherd" and Jesus is "The Door" of the sheep. He is the way in, and He is the sovereign protector for those who enter. Twice Jesus intimates that His purpose in coming was to lay down His life for His sheep. Obviously the cross did not take Him by surprise. He came to die on the cross. Of special interest, however, in this passage is His reference to the fact that no one can take His life from Him. He said He had the power to lay it down and to take it up again (verse 18). No one else who ever lived ever dared to make such a statement. And only Jesus Christ fulfilled it. He is the only One Who ever came back from death to demonstrate that He could. But the fact that no one could take His life from Him is as important as that He could take it up again. Jesus was invulnerable to death by His own admission. Except He Himself were willing to lay down His life, it could not be taken from Him.

How did He die then when He hung on the Cross? The answer is, He died by the sheer, deliberate act of His own will. He literally laid down His life for His sheep. "For this purpose I have come to this hour."—John 12:27 (R.S.V.)

❖❖❖❖❖❖❖❖❖❖❖

Spend some time thinking about the first six verses of this passage. The analogy of sheep and shepherd is a beautiful picture of the relation between Christ and the believer. Why do the sheep follow the shepherd (verse 4), why does any man follow Christ? Who do you suppose are meant in verse 16?

"You Gotta Show Me"

John 14:1-11

This passage is one of the most familiar, primarily because it is so often used in funerals. But there is much more to this than mere comfort in time of sorrow. Here is recorded one of the most significant conversations between Jesus and His disciples. Incidentally, the Apostle Thomas is interesting at this point. He did not believe easily. He was incredulous toward Jesus. Like a Missourian, he had to be shown. Because of this, the familiar phrase "doubting Thomas" was coined. But the important point is that here is demonstrated the fact that Jesus is quite ready to resolve honest doubts when men are willing to see. Jesus honors the man who "has to be shown."

Furthermore, it is often out of doubts like these that the most precious truth comes to light. (Some folks never doubt because they never think—they just rearrange their prejudices). Had it not been for Thomas' doubt and Philip's dissatisfaction, we would have missed some tremendous truth.

Take one word out of verse 6, the word "way." Jesus did not say, "I am the way-shower." He said, "I am the way . . . " All other religious leaders were way-showers, Jesus claimed to be THE WAY! In the original language, the word translated "way" means literally "road." Whereas the road takes a man to his destination, the signs along the highway only point the direction. Other great teachers pointed a way . . . Jesus IS THE way! "You believe in God— believe also in me . . ."—John 14:1.

❖❖❖❖❖❖❖❖❖❖❖❖

Words like those of verses 1-3 take the sting out of death. Whatever Jesus meant by them, we can be sure the man who trusts in Him has nothing to fear of dying. Examine the exchange between Jesus and Philip. What do you get out of this rather startling declaration by Jesus? Compare verse 9 with the last half of verse 6.

The Verdict Is Yours

John 18:12—19:16

Many books have been written by lawyers about the famous trial recorded in this portion of Scripture. It was conducted in the early hours of the morning as evidenced by the rooster's crow signaling the dawn (18:27). If ever a trial was a travesty of justice, this was. It vividly portrays the blindness and hardness and inflexibility of unbelief ("Don't disturb me with the facts, I've already made up my mind.").

Why did they crucify Jesus? The best evidence they could muster was false and their case fell apart in court. Yet, though three men (Annas, Caiaphas, Pilate) tried Him, who were supposed to represent not only civil, but religious justice, He was found guilty. This is the way unbelief works—rejection of evidence.

In every generation since that consummate mistrial, men have tried Jesus and, though lacking evidence, have condemned Him. The deceptions that men invent and devise to discredit Jesus would be laughable if the infidelity of their intellectual facade was not so tragic—so heartbreaking. It is really pitiful the way intelligent men try to get rid of Jesus Christ! Their deception is so transparent one finds it difficult to see how they can take it so seriously.

Actually, Jesus was not on trial! Human nature was! It is incumbent upon every man to decide what to do with Jesus. This is an inescapable verdict facing each man, and the eternal welfare of his soul depends upon his vote. To be undecided is to be against Jesus, (John 3:18) and to decide against Jesus is to be condemned. "He who believes in the Son has eternal life; he who does not obey the Son shall not see life, but the wrath of God rests upon him."—John 3:36 (RSV)

❖❖❖❖❖❖❖❖❖❖❖❖

In the context of the above passage, it would be enlightening to study 2 Corinthians 4:3-4. Did you notice in John 3:18 the relationship between the words "believe" and "disobey?"

Man In Christ

Man As He Is By Nature... And Grace

Ephesians 2:1-10

Christianity is primarily a matter of life or death, not right or wrong, goodness or badness. The Christian is a good man in the accepted sense, but a non-Christian may be a good man also. Christianity involves ethics, but it goes infinitely deeper than ethics. Ethics has to do with conduct, Christianity deals with a man's nature. Christianity is concerned with what a man is, not just what he does! *Christianity is life, not ethics.*

Therefore it gives a man more than moral principles by which to live, it equips him with the power of a new life. It literally means that the power of Christ Himself is resident in the Christian. For this reason the genuinely Christian man has supernatural equipment with which to meet life's problems. He is meant to be the master, never the victim of his circumstances.

This is absolutely basic to the understanding of

Christian faith. The non-Christian has a wrong nature! Though his conduct may be acceptable, his basic nature is wrong (Mark 7:14-23). Outwardly he may look fine, but inwardly is where the trouble lurks. This is the explanation for the downfall of so many "good" men. They hadn't learned to deal with a nature which was deceitful at its best—a nature which had the ability to behave itself at one time and act like the devil another. This is why the good man gone wrong cannot explain himself except to say, "I don't know why I did it. I don't know why I did it!" Of course, he doesn't, because he allowed himself to be deceived about himself. Wanting to believe the best about himself, he took seriously that teaching which congratulated human nature on how fine and respectable it is.

This is the fundamental deceptive streak in human goodness. It seeks to be mollified rather than to be exposed. Man does not like the truth about himself. Like the man who will not submit to a routine physical examination fearing what might be discovered, so human goodness refuses to expose itself to writing or teaching or preaching which does more than massage the ego. ("This is the condemnation, that light is come into the world and men loved darkness more than light because their deeds were evil." John 3:19)

This is the reason some "good" men refuse to attend church. They prefer to go on blissfully ignorant of what's inside human nature that makes them do the crazy things they do.

Ephesians 2:1-10 is basic Christianity. Here is the truth of God about man together with the provision God has made for man's need. The first three verses state the problem, the Divine diagnosis, and verses 4 through 9 give the solution, the Divine prescription. Verse 10 is a summation and the distilled essence of Christianity in a sentence.

❖❖❖❖❖❖❖❖❖❖❖

What are the characteristics of the unregenerate man as described in Ephesians 2:1-3? What does God do to remedy this condition? What is the definition of a Christian according to verse 10?

Truth Through Personality

John 1:1-14

The first fourteen verses of John's Gospel are commonly called the prologue. That is, they contain an introduction to the Gospel and a summary of its total message. But they are more than that for in these verses is contained in a capsule the whole plan of God to meet man's need.

Two verses are especially significant for your consideration. Verse 14 declares that God actually invaded history in the Person of His Son (compare verses 1-3 with 14). Verse 12 gives the application of the solution.

It is one thing for a physician to prescribe medication, another thing for a man to take it. The finest medical science, the best medications, are useless if a man refuses to take them. God has provided a solution, but it is up to man to receive it. It is not that Christianity has been tried and found wanting . . . but rather that it has not really been tried. "Jesus answered and said unto him, 'Verily, verily I say unto you, except a man be born again, he cannot see the kingdom of God.' "—John 3:3.

✦✦✦✦✦✦✦✦✦✦✦✦

What are the qualities attributed to the "Word" in the first five verses? On the basis of verses 12 and 13, how does one become a son of God? According to verse 14, what method did God use for the supreme and final revelation of Himself?

Religion Is Not Enough

John 3:1-16

There is a difference between religion and Christianity! We might as well face it. Nicodemus was undoubtedly one of the most honorable men of his day. He was a Pharisee, which speaks for his serious religious outlook and commitment (they were the strictest sect of the Jews). He was a "ruler of the Jews" which speaks of his position, his superior wisdom, his integrity, his leadership. He was a far-above-the-average man. He was a member of the Sanhedrin, the highest court of Jewry—equivalent to our Supreme Court. He was certainly a moral man whose public and private life was above reproach. Furthermore, he was more than curious about Jesus, hence this private interview.

The facts are interesting: A brilliant, devoutly religious, highly ethical leader of the Jews confronting Jesus Christ. Nicodemus discovers among other things that his religion and morality are not enough . . . he needs something else (he must have sensed

109

this about himself, consequently he sought out Jesus). Jesus said what he needed was a new birth. "Born again?" What kind of a conundrum is this? "How can a man be born when he is old?" It's a valid question and deserves a straight answer. The way in which Jesus handles this is rather interesting.

The discussion which ensues culminates in what is commonly called the "Golden Text" of the Bible (verse 16). Rare is the American who has not memorized this verse in childhood. It sums up God's total answer to man's total need. If men refuse God's Son, they will refuse anything God offers! *Whatever a man needs for life now and forever, that need is met in Jesus Christ, the Son of God.* That is the supreme affirmation of Christianity! The heart of Christianity is not an ethical code, nor a theological system, but a PERSON! "For God sent not his Son into the world to condemn the world, but that the world through Him might be saved."—John 3:17

❖❖❖❖❖❖❖❖❖❖❖❖

No man was more qualified than Nicodemus to by-pass Christianity. But he too needed to learn the secret of life eternal, that it involves more than religious practice, more than moral and ethical living . . . it involves a man's relation to a Person. Jesus Christ is more than religion, infinitely more! Incidentally, Nicodemus became a follower of Jesus, secretly at first, finally out in the open. What do you get out of Jesus' explanation of the new birth?

A Gift Must Be Received

John 3:16-21

There are two sides to a gift, giving and receiving. Both are required to complete the gift. Nothing is more humiliating to the giver than to have his gift ignored or refused. Nothing is more insulting to a giver than rejection! He cannot force a gift, he can only offer it.

"God so loved that He gave . . ." That is the heart of Christianity, the heart of the Hebrew-Christian tradition, the heart of the Bible—a loving God, a giving God! This love of God's, this gift of God's distinguishes Christianity from all other religions. God gave, man is intended to receive.

Reduced to its simple terms, the message of the Bible is this loving and giving of God to man. And the supreme tragedy is man's perennial failure to receive this love, this gift.

Christmas, for example, means comparatively little more than a headache, extra bills and exhaustion to the man who has not responded to God's love and received His gift. To this man Christmas is incomplete, only half a transaction. And when Christmas is over, God is left holding His priceless gift, unacceptable, declined. Imagine one lonely gift left under the tree, unclaimed. Days pass and the tree must be thrown out. The gift is still there. Nobody will take it. What a scar on the heart of the one who gave the gift, what a rebuff to the loving care with which it was selected with a beloved recipient in mind. But there it lies, unwanted. Nothing to do but throw it out with the tree.

The coming of the Son of God into history by way of the virgin birth was meant to be more than an isolated event of history, it was meant to be a personal encounter for man. Jesus' entrance into history was only the first phase of redemption, the second phase is His acceptance by men that He might abide in them, reign in their hearts as Lord.

Is Christmas a personal experience for you, or simply a perfunctory celebration of an event 1900 years old which has no relevance in your life? You can make it personal and relevant by receiving the Son of God now. "To as many as received Him, to them He gave the power to become the sons of God . . ."—John 1:12.

❖❖❖❖❖❖❖❖❖❖❖❖

According to this passage of Scripture, who is condemned? Who is not condemned? Why is a man condemned? What is the indictment? What was the purpose of the coming of the Son of God?

A New Man

2 Corinthians 5:16-21

Christianity is infinitely more than reformation. It is regeneration by the power of almighty God. Being Christian is not something man does for himself, nor for his fellowman, nor for God. *Being Christian is something God does to and in and for man.* God makes the Christian, not man. Higher than the heaven above the earth is God's regeneration above man's reformation. Mere moral reformation does not explain the true Christian. He can be explained only in terms of God's transforming power which makes man literally a new creation. Christianity is not man beginning over . . . it is God beginning in man a work of which man himself is utterly incapable.

Christianity is God giving to man that which is utterly outside man, which he does not have except God gives it to him. Christianity is God's righteousness, Divine perfection, offered to man in the person of Jesus Christ. "To as many as received Him (Christ) to them He gave the power to become the Sons of God, even to those who believed on his name, who were born . . . of God."—John 1:12-13

❖❖❖❖❖❖❖❖❖❖❖

Think through 2 Corinthians 5:17. What meaning does this have for you? As you evaluate your own Christian experience, is it simply you trying to do your best, or have you received something "eternal" from God?

Goodness Vs. Godliness

Luke 5:17-32

One of the most effective satanic devices is the concept that sin is limited to vice as contrasted with virtue. The man who thinks this way equates virtue with righteousness, ethics becomes the substance of his religion, and the step from ethics to irreligion is a relatively short one. For it does not take a perceptive man long to discover that he can live a moderately ethical life without the help of religion. He finds himself doing as well as the man who seems to take religion quite seriously.

Going to church becomes an imposition to the man who is legitimately busy all week, especially when he feels that in the main he has conducted himself as an ethical man should. He needs Sunday to rest and recreate. Why should he tie himself down to a church service? Failing to see any real benefit in church attendance, he simply quits, and utilizes Sunday morning in ways he feels are more productive.

On this basis the good man is the Christian man
. . . and goodness in fact becomes the greatest foe of
authentic Christianity. His own goodness becomes
that which draws a man from the church, the Bible
and Christ.

This caricature is not peculiar to the twentieth
century. It was true in Jesus' day and it has been
true in every generation of human history. It was
the "good" people, indeed, the "religious" people
of Jesus' day who repudiated Him and saw to His
liquidation. Thus goodness has been the supreme opponent to Godliness from the dawn of history, when
Eve allowed herself to be enticed away from obedience to God by the temptation to be like God on
her own.

Vice is the result of sin—the effect, the fruit, not
the root. The root of sin is man's self-alienation from
God, man becomes his own god. The essence of
so-called "original sin" is this: man, though made
for God and to have fellowship with God, declares
his independence from God and lives on that basis.
The supreme expression of man's spiritual rebellion
in history is man's attempt to imitate God while he
remains independently his own god in his own
affairs. This spiritual insubordination is the root of
sin, the embryo of evil in history.

Having separated himself from God, man must

find a way to defend himself against a return to God, and the most self-satisfying defense he can make is a good life, which makes God, for all practical purposes, unnecessary. Not that he doesn't believe in God. Of course he does. After all, he's not a heathen. But as far as ethics is concerned, he gets along very nicely without ever giving God a thought. So man's goodness becomes a neat little defense mechanism against God. "And the Pharisees and their scribes murmured against His disciples, saying, 'Why do you eat and drink with tax collectors and sinners?' And Jesus answered them, 'Those who are well have no need of a physician, but those who are sick; I have not come to call the righteous, but sinners to repentance.' "—Luke 5:30-32. (R.S.V.)

✻✻✻✻✻✻✻✻✻✻✻✻

The Pharisees didn't catch on! They were so saturated with their own self-righteousness and complacency that they were impervious to the gentle sarcasm of Jesus. Most of them missed the point Jesus kept trying to make, ie. that He couldn't help the man who didn't think he needed any help. Consider the verses 17-24 carefully. What do you make of these unusual statements my Jesus?

Authentic Goodness

The test of goodness is what it does when it is confronted by Jesus Christ! Viewed objectively, it is inconceivable that a truly good man could oppose Jesus Christ. After all, Jesus was the personification of goodness. He was perfection incarnate! He was the quintessence of virtue! There must be some fundamental flaw in a professed goodness that would be offended in Jesus or repudiate Him.

The real enemies of Jesus were without exception men who professed goodness, but as the events of His life unfold, their vaunted goodness becomes increasingly transparent and the hypocrisy of their lives is exposed. The sheer integrity of Jesus' life was a stinging rebuke to them and a judgment upon their deceit. Every calculated effort they made to discredit Him ended in their own confounding and confusion until they were beside themselves with jealousy and rage. Trace the cumulative effect of

Jesus' moral perfection upon their lives and you see the difference between authentic goodness and the counterfeit man calls by that name.

Every once in awhile in the record you come across a man who is genuinely good though he is not a disciple of Jesus. Such is the case in the Scripture under consideration. The authenticity of his goodness becomes apparent when he encounters Jesus.

There is nothing particularily unusual about the man in our story. He is a centurion, which means he was a professional soldier, and an eminently successful one at that. Roman soldiers were notably hard and secular. This man had heard of Jesus, but he had never met Him. He knew the facts about Jesus' life . . . the same facts which Jesus' enemies knew but refused to accept. He was curious and interested and what's more he had a kind of faith in Jesus, a sort of faith at a distance.

As you read the narrative, you become aware of a strength of character about this man, an element that is noticeably lacking in the Pharisees who were so insufferably self-confident. He is really a good man. Look what the Jews have to say to Jesus about him. See how earnestly they beseech Jesus to meet him and help him. Observe the remarkable response of the centurion as Jesus draws near.

Notable also is this man's faith. A man of authority himself, he appreciates authority in another. He entertained not the slightest doubt that Jesus had authority to do whatsoever He would do! You will notice that Jesus commends this recognition as remarkable faith, a faith to be emulated. Jesus said, "I tell you, I have not found so great faith, no, not in Israel." Verse 9.

❖❖❖❖❖❖❖❖❖❖❖❖

Contrast the attitude of this centurion with the Pharisee in Luke 18:9-14. What difference do you see in these two men? Do we have a right to suspect a man who outwardly seems to be a good man yet who stubbornly refuses to have anything to do with Jesus? What is the explanation for the rejection of Jesus by seemingly good men?

The Good Secular Man

Luke 12:13-21

Be careful not to read into this story what is not there. Give this successful farmer the benefit of the doubt. He is undoubtedly to be commended for his industry, his efficiency, his integrity. Nothing in the parable suggests that he came by his wealth wrongly. He probably paid his help well and was kind to his neighbors and family. He was simply a wise farmer who planned carefully, worked hard, and profited abundantly.

He might have been what used to be called in the rich agricultural belts of the eastern seaboard, a "master farmer." The master farmer was a leading citizen of his community, respected, admired, emulated. Generally he was on the board of the local bank, often its president, he was usually a member of the school board and more often than not, an officer in the local church.

So far as the record is concerned, the man in our

story was simply a good man who had left God entirely out of his life. Not that he was an atheist, he just lived as though God were not important. He made his plans without the slightest sense of his accountability to God, without a shred of gratitude to the One Who made the soil and weather smile on his efforts as a farmer. He gave himself total credit for his success. He was soaked in secularism! He was a good, Godless man!

In this prosperous farmer, we see the ultimate in the secular spirit: the illusion that security is found in things, that life equals possessions, that a good man is sufficient on his own. God calls such a man a fool! "Where your treasure is, there will your heart be."

❖❖❖❖❖❖❖❖❖❖❖

Though you wouldn't express it this crudely (verse 19), do you treat your soul this way? What are you feeding your soul? What kind of nourishment do you serve your spirit? What would you say about this man's solution to his surpluses?

The Good Man's Criticism Of Jesus

Luke 15:1-30

One thing which made Jesus an enigma to the religous people of His day was the fact that disreputable men and women were attracted to Him, followed Him, spent hours listening to Him. But what was even more exasperating, Jesus did not drive them away or disassociate Himself from them. On the contrary, He fraternized with them, seemed almost to delight in their company.

This the religionists simply could not "stomach." They were "separatists." They disassociated themselves from the world, drew their self-righteous robes about themselves and kept their distance from the "scum." Their religion provided them with a handy insulation against the desperate misery and need around them. What's more, they could justify it in the name of *separation.* They wouldn't soil their hands.

On the other hand, Jesus welcomed sinners to

123

Himself. Again and again He answered the criticism of the religionists by trying to make them understand that His whole purpose in coming into the world was to help sinners, to save them. His business was redemption! He had come to "lift men from the miry pit, to set their feet upon a rock and establish their goings." As the sick needed a physician, so the sinner needed Him. The Pharisees, unable or unwilling to comprehend this, labelled Jesus a "drunkard, glutton and winebibber." There is a sense in which the Church is like a hospital for the sick souls, she is certainly not an organization of people who have achieved perfection.

Jesus' answer to their criticism in this instance took the form of three parables. Each of the parables has to do with a lost something or someone. The point of the parables is found in verses 7, 10, 22-24, 32. Verse 7 contains one of the most daring statements of the mercy of God to be found in the Bible. Think on this verse until you see it. "The Son of Man is not come to call the righteous, but sinners to repentance."

❊❊❊❊❊❊❊❊❊❊❊❊

Why did Jesus tell *three* parables? Is there a difference in the "lostness" of the three stories? If so, what is the difference, and what application should be made?

The Misguided Prayer
Of A Good Man

Luke 18:9-14

One danger is that we judge too harshly the Pharisee in this story. He is simply reflecting the truth about all men who have the idea they are good enough without faith in Christ. But this is one of the clever defenses that the "good" man makes to cover his own need. By some strange perversity within him, he feels he justifies his own failure by indignation over the failure of others. When Jesus says, "Judge not that ye be not judged," He is laying down a sound psychological principle, ie., that *we generally condemn in others that which we find in ourselves.* So don't treat the Pharisee in this story as though he is a rare specimen, unlike most of us.

Nothing is more modern than the ethical, twentieth century American who, because of his respectability, thinks of himself as far superior to the man on skidrow, for example. This is one of the deceptions in human goodness. It breeds the "superior" man. Because he does not do what another does, he thinks of himself as a superior person, and his sense of superiority is the worst sin, for it is pride, the root sin.

Whatever else is true of the genuinely good person, he is humble and grateful to God for His mercy. The truly good man realizes that but for the grace of God he would be down in the mud like some of the pitiable fallen men he sees in the gutter. He's not proud, he's thankful!

Think of the Apostle Paul, the greatest of the Apostles, who wrote more than half of the New Testament, who was the first Christian missionary planting the Church throughout Asia Minor and Europe. This brilliant, Christ-like, dedicated Apostle called himself "the chief of sinners" and "less than the least of all saints."

Incidentally, Roget's TREASURY OF WORDS gives as synonyms for "respectable" such words as "so and so," "average," "moderate," "mediocre."

"And when you pray, you must not be like the hypocrites; for they love to stand and pray in the synagogues and at the street corners, that they may be seen by men. Truly, I say to you, they have their reward."—Matthew 6:5. (R.S.V.)

❉❉❉❉❉❉❉❉❉❉❉

THE MISGUIDED PRAYER OF A GOOD MAN

There is a vivid description of two predominant characteristics of pride in human goodness given in Luke 18:9. What are these two characteristics? With whom did the Pharisee pray (verse 11)? Why was the tax collector justified rather than the Pharisee?

The Good Man Who Lacked Something

Did Jesus oppose capitalism? Did He teach that wealth was evil? These verses have been used to prove that He did. But it is a terrible abuse of the Scriptures to impose such an interpretation upon it.

Did Jesus deny equality with God? This same passage has been used to prove that also, and again it is an abuse of the passage. As a matter of fact, one has but to study the story carefully in context to see that Jesus was actually intimating His equality with God.

Both of these abuses will be considered in due time, but first, the meat of the narrative.

Here was a wealthy man whose life, so far as his fellow man was concerned, was unimpeachable. He must have been an attractive person because the record of this same incident in another Gospel adds the fact that "Jesus, looking on him, loved him." This isn't said about many contacts of Jesus. This man had had an excellent rearing in a devout home. So successful had his parental training been that he could say honestly and frankly, "I have kept all these commandments from my youth." That is a stupendous claim to make, especially standing in front of Jesus. The Lord knew this about him too, and was undoubtedly impressed with such a clean, sharp, keen model of manhood. This man was not hypocritical or proud, he was simply stating a fact. But he lacked something and he knew it, or he would never have bothered Jesus with the question.

What did he lack?

Notice the commandments which Jesus listed. The ten commandments divide into two parts: the first four to do with man's obligation to God, the last six have to do with man's obligation to his fellow man (See Matthew 22:37). Jesus did not mention the first four commandments because He wanted to emphasize in a concrete way to this man, his utter lack of awareness of his Godward obligation. So Jesus went directly to the heart of the problem, putting His finger right on the deficiency in his life.

Jesus instructed the man to sell his possessions and give them to the poor so he would have treasure in heaven. But the man went away sorrowful, for he was a "very rich man." Instead of discussing a theological theory about God and a man's duty to

Him, Jesus gave this man a choice between treasure in heaven and treasure on earth. Immediately it became clear that his wealth was his god. If he had to choose between his wealth and God, he would choose wealth.

Here was an ethical man who made the secular choice. He was a good, Godless man!

Did Jesus oppose capitalism? He did not! His parable of the talents teach capitalism. The servant who had five talents was commended for doubling his investment as was also the servant who had two talents. The servant with one talent was soundly rebuked and his talent was taken away, not because he had not made as much as the others, but because he had made nothing. He had buried his talent instead of putting it to work.

But did Jesus teach that wealth was evil in the story we've been discussing? After all, did He not say, "it is easier for a camel to go through the eye of a needle than for a man to enter the Kingdom of God." He did say that, but the reaction of those who heard it sheds some light on what he meant. They said, "Then who can be saved?" Now if this had been a matter of riches being evil per se, you would have expected those who heard it to say, "Whew, that leaves us out, we're not rich, we're poor." Instead they included themselves in the same predicament with the rich man. Then Jesus replied, "What is impossible with men is possible with God." *The danger of trust in mammon is the point.* Sometimes the poor man is more preoccupied with money than the rich man. Sometimes the man who has little or nothing worships the "almighty dollar" more than the man who has much.

Incidentally, another important fact is born out here, ie., the impossibility of man saving himself. Only God can save!

Did Jesus repudiate equality with God here? When the man addressed Him as "Good Master . . . ," Jesus said to him, "Why callest thou me good? None is good, save God . . ." This sounds as though Jesus is refusing the salutation. On the contrary, Jesus is testing the man's sincerity. Why does this man call Him good? Because he recognizes Him as God, or because he is patronizing Him? Is this salutation sincere, or is it hypocritical? Jesus categorically rejected patronage. He insisted on being worshipped! See Luke 19:37-40. By the way, Jesus' question concerning the salutation indicates His estimate of goodness.

❖❖❖❖❖❖❖❖❖❖❖❖

Read Matthew 22:37. What is the first and great commandment? Of what is a man guilty who does not keep it?

The Enigma Of The Cross

Matthew 27:32-54

When you really think it through, the cross of Jesus is the most enigmatic fact of history! It defies explanation on any reasonable grounds.

Jesus was human in every sense of the word, subject to weariness, privation, temptation, yet never giving in, never yielding. He was human nature at its outside best. History records no trace of weakness, sin or selfishness in Him. He was the epitome of virtue. He was honesty, selflessness, goodness incarnate. He literally spent Himself for others, never accumulated a thing, never indulged a moment satisfying selfish desires or ambitions. He was a perfect man!

Yet His contemporaries crucified Him as a common criminal. To the everlasting shame of humanity, it crucified the only perfect representative of itself. (This is the history of humanity—righteousness on a cross) The cross was the most despised form of capital punishment. It was so terrible that a Roman citizen could not be crucified, no matter what his crime. It was reserved for the worst offenders, crime's worst penalty. The fanatical enemies of Jesus were forced to employ false witnesses. Their case fell apart in court. Pilate could find "no fault in Him." He said Jesus was a "just person," yet he let Him be crucified. Pilate was insufferably weak.

What made crucifixion so horrible was that it meant death from sheer exhaustion, body dehydration. Normally it took several days. Jesus was on the cross only a few hours. Roman guards were staggered by the suddenness of His death. What killed Him? Why did He die so soon?

The cross didn't kill Him. He was not on it long enough. When you comprehend the death of Jesus, you have the key to the whole plan of God for the salvation of humanity. The cross is the clue, the core, the crux of the plan.

In his impatience, Pilate said, "Do you not know that I have the power to release you, the power to crucify you?" Jesus answered, "You have no power over Me at all. . ." Another time he said, "No man taketh my life from Me, I have the power to lay it down and I have the power to take it up again." They didn't take His life from Him. Nothing they could have done would have accomplished this. "In Him was life." He was the Author, the Source of life. Life originated with Him.

He laid down His life by the sheer act of His will. He literally "laid down" His life. From the cross He cried "Finished!"

What was finished? The thing He had come to do. He came to die on the cross. He was "the lamb of God that taketh away the sin of the world." He laid down His life for humanity. "Without the shedding of blood is no remission of sin."—Hebrews 9:22.

❋❋❋❋❋❋❋❋❋❋❋

There are two studies relative to the cross of Jesus which are very interesting and profitable. One is an examination of the events that accompanied His death. Examine this passage in terms of the unusual phenomena which occurred as He died. Second, is a study of the things Jesus said as He hung on the cross, the so-called "Seven last words." Consider the things He spoke as He hung there.

Easter, Fact Or Fiction?

Matthew 28:1-15

Easter is not the expression of some fond but vain anticipation, some incredible ethereal hope unfulfilled. It is the celebration of a cosmic historical fact, the actual, literal, bodily resurrection of Jesus from the grave.

Late Thursday night, first century, A. D., they took Him prisoner while He was praying in Gethsemane. At the home of Annas and Caiaphas, He was perfunctorily tried and condemned. Early Friday morning, just as it began to dawn, they took Him bound to the Praetorium where Pilate, provincial Governor, ruled. Between Herod and Pilate there ensued a series of ridiculous, diabolical prostitutions of justice which ended with Jesus condemned to death by crucifixion.

The penalty was instantly carried out. In a few hours His broken body hung limp and dead on the cross. They took it down, wrapped it in burial linen, put it in a tomb, rolled a huge stone over the entrance, applied the official seal of Imperial Rome, stationed a platoon of guards. Early Sunday morning, some of His disciples came to the tomb. To their shock and chagrin, the tomb was empty. The stone was removed, the seal broken, the body gone, although the wrappings remained in the shape of the body on the slab in the tomb.

Where was the body? The enemies of Jesus would have paid any price to recover it. It would have established once and for all their claim that He was an imposter. Their only recourse was to pay the Roman soldiers to lie, say that the body had been stolen by His disciples while they slept. What a lie, if they were asleep, how would they know what had happened? The stupid efforts men make to discredit the truth!

It was no fiction, it was solid fact! Jesus had risen from the dead as He said He would. They didn't believe Him—even His disciples disbelieved. So it was no illusion when they saw Him, though when He first appeared they thought He was a ghost. He proved to the contrary by letting them handle Him, feel His flesh and bone, put a finger in the nail holes in his hands. He ate their food. Ghosts don't eat fish and bread. This was real! For forty days He walked the earth, showed Himself alive by "many infallible proofs." He appeared to many, including more than five hundred on one occasion.

The resurrection fact is thoroughly substantiated by evidence. No fact of history stands more completely verified. *Jesus Christ is not a dead martyr, He is a living, contemporary Saviour!* He is alive today, a reality in the experience of Christmas. He defeated man's worst enemy, death, robbed victory from the grave. He has life to offer, eternal life. It is a gift for all who will have it. You cannot earn it, but you can receive it without price. "God so loved the world that He gave His only begotten Son . . ." —John 3:16.

✳✳✳✳✳✳✳✳✳✳✳✳

Sometime for an interesting experiment, examine the arguments scholars in every age have put forth in their strange effort to discredit the fact of the bodily resurrection of Jesus. See if any of these scholars give one shred of evidence for their theories. See if it is not much easier to believe the facts as they are recorded in the New Testament than to accept the transparent inventions designed to replace the facts.

A Loose, Much-Married Woman — And Jesus

John 4:7-42

One woman, and five husbands! Quite a record, even for modern times.

And to make matters worse, this woman was now living with a man who was not her husband. Her presence would be quite unacceptable to conventional folk, she would probably not receive a very warm welcome from many church people. She was undoubtedly accustomed to the rejection of the "proper" set.

But significantly, it was this woman with whom Jesus stopped to chat, in whom He took special interest. Notwithstanding the fact that He knew all about her and knew furthermore, the criticism which would be provoked by his familiarity with her. No self-respecting Jew conversed publicly with any woman, least of all a Samaritan, a despised half-gentile. Nevertheless, Jesus engaged her. Asking for a drink was merely His way of bidding for her con-

fidence so He could do for her what He knew
needed to be done.

Gently, patiently He brought her around to the
place where she opened her heart to Him, confessed
her sin and shame and underwent the revolutionary
change in her life which submission to Jesus Christ
produces. Not only she, but her whole village felt
the impact. She ran to tell them of this fascinating
Person Who had told her "all things whatsoever I
did." They saw and felt the change in her. This
much-married, loose-living woman was a new person. Her testimony was irresistible. They followed
her to see this fantastic man, who not only had the
insight of a seer but could transform the personality
of a fallen woman. They too saw and heard. They
too believed, no longer because of the change in the
woman, but because they had seen Jesus for themselves, and were convinced, and changed.

Two things bear consideration: (1) Jesus was
interested in people we are inclined to think of as
beyond hope. As a physican is interested in the sick,
Jesus was interested in those whose lives were bankrupt. His mission was to such. He still seeks those
who need Him today. He is always available. The
only condition He requires is that a man come to
Him admitting his need. (2) It is not necessary to
get by on a second-hand faith. Valid as was the

testimony of the woman, the clincher was Jesus Christ Himself. Don't be satisfied with anything less than your own first-hand experience of the contemporary Christ. "Behold I stand at the door and knock. If any man hear my voice and open the door, I will come in to him and sup with him and he with me."—Revelation 3:20.

❖❖❖❖❖❖❖❖❖❖❖

This is the longest of Jesus' conversations with an individual recorded in the New Testament. It contains the best example of His counselling with one person. There is much we can learn from this incident. He made contact by asking a favor and then gently, but steadily led her to divulge her need. The truth stated in verses 13-15 is timely for the insatiable thirst of our modern generation. *Nothing satisfies like Christ.*

CHAPTER

FIVE

The Knowledgeable Man

The Wise Builder

Matthew 7:24-27

This is being written in beautiful Hawaii. As I write, there is much activity outside my hotel room window. Kaiser is building an addition to his Hawaiian Village Hotel. With great care the workmen are laying the foundation for a seventeen story building.

Neglect at this point might be at the expense of the superstructure later. Everything about a building depends upon its foundation. The wise builder looks well to the undergirding.

This is just as true of man. The foundation on which he builds his life is absolutely essential to the future of that life. Yet men are prone to overlook this. Putting all their energy and effort into the visible part of themselves, they ignore the foundation. Floods come—they are inevitable, and the life is imperiled by reverses, troubles, tragedies. No matter how good the materials that went into the superstructure and regardless of the care with which the man built, the life may collapse.

Jesus said a man was like a fool building on sand if he disregarded His teaching. Don't get so preoccupied with life that you neglect the foundation. "Other foundation can no man lay, than that is laid, which is Jesus Christ.—1 Corinthians 3:11.

✤✤✤✤✤✤✤✤✤✤✤

Stop to think about this remarkable declaration Jesus made. No wonder they were amazed as He taught, for He spoke with authority. Who else in history would dare to make such a categorical claim for his teaching?

The Wise Man
And The Fool

Proverbs 1:1-19

"The best guide to success a young man can have."
So one describes the book of Proverbs. It is a young
man's counsellor, abounding in practical, down-to-
earth wisdom. Concentrated in these brief thirty-
one chapters is a library of shrewd, practical common sense. It has been said that "Christianity is the
perfection of common sense," and in Proverbs we
see the distilled essence of Christian wisdom. Con-
veniently the book is divided into thirty-one chapters, making it possible to read one a day and complete it in a month.

A proverb is a "short, pithy, axiomatic saying, the
truth of which is emphasized by contrasting statements." Most of the Proverbs were written by Solomon and should a man entertain any doubt as to the
unusual wisdom of this ancient king of Israel, let
him try to compose just one proverb. Proverbs deals
with ethical and moral wisdom shedding light on

144

the daily affairs. Many of the verses lend themselves easily to memorizing.

The first nineteen verses form an introduction to the whole book. Here Solomon sets forth his object: to promote wisdom, instruction, understanding, righteousness, equity, prudence, knowledge, discretion, learning. The thesis of the book is that true wisdom is based upon a right relationship to God. There is knowledge, "the getting of which makes man ignorant and foolish." There is a kind of knowledge which draws a man farther from God and leads to deeper and deeper stupidity, a kind of knowledge which makes a man less and less wise in his day to day affairs. Such is the knowledge that is not founded upon fear (respect or reverence) of God. Proverbs sets forth Godly wisdom. Its teaching is dependable, practical, workable, edifying. "The fear of the Lord is the beginning of wisdom."

❖❖❖❖❖❖❖❖❖❖❖❖

Significant throughout Proverbs is the assumption that the counsel of parents is to be trusted (1:8-9). Is this a safe assumption today? Examine 1:24-25, man's deliberate rejection of God's wisdom and 1:28-31, the inevitable consequence of such rejection.

Much Which Adds Up To Nothing

Proverbs 13

Living faith in God is more than just a "passport to heaven." It is a way of life here and now. It is the way of maximum personal efficiency and productivity. The accusation that Christianity is a "pie-in-the-sky-by-and-by" deal could not be further from the truth. It involves the eternal welfare of a man, to be sure, but it also involves the next moment of his life, and each succeeding moment thereafter, forever. The sober fact is that man becomes what he really believes and indifference toward God or rebellion to His truth triggers destructive consequences, not just in terms of life after death, but right now, in the present.

Of course a man can get along without God, or seem to at any rate, without any apparent evil results, just like a man can jump from a tall building and suffer no ill effects . . . until he hits the pavement. The only difference is the immediacy of discernable consequences. In the case of breaking the law of gravity, it is more sudden than when breaking the spiritual and moral law. But the thing never to forget is the fact that consequences are immediate, if not noticeable, and cumulative in the man who is indifferent to God. "Despisest thou the riches of His goodness and forbearance and longsuffering; not knowing that the goodness of God leadeth thee to repentance? But after thy hardness and impenitent heart treasurest up unto thyself wrath against the day of wrath and revelation of the righteous judgment of God . . ."—Romans 2:4-5.

❖❖❖❖❖❖❖❖❖❖❖❖

God doesn't settle accounts at the end of the day. In His longsuffering and patience He waits for man to recognize His goodness and mercy. Notice verse 11, it does make a difference how a man gets his wealth. As an end in itself, wealth is always destructive.

The Power Of The Tongue

Proverbs 18

Who can measure the damage done by careless conversation, not to mention the sheer destruction wrought by the one whose tongue is deliberately evil. Recurring in Proverbs is the counsel regarding a man's speech. It would be profitable to examine James 3:2-13 as collateral reading. In this context note the last verse of the preceding proverb.

Who of us has not wanted to bite off his tongue when he has said something impetuously or harshly. The experience of each of us makes us appreciate the wisdom of God concerning the tongue. A man may regret his silence on occasion, but more often does he regret his conversation. At least there's nothing to "take back" from silence. There is the story of one whose tongue was always wagging and whose words injured many good people. Convicted in her conscience of the crime of gossip, she sought a counsellor. The irreparable, irretrievable nature of words when spoken was graphically illustrated as the counsellor asked the woman to imagine trying to collect the feathers from a pillow after they had been scattered by the wind. Words too, can never be taken back. We may apologize and repent and try to make amends, but the words can never be made to return to the tongue, nor can their bitter hurt be removed. "Words unspoken on the tongue, often drop back dead; but even God Himself cannot stop a word, when it's been said."

One thing certain, a man is never learning when his mouth is open speaking. "It is one thing to be thought a fool, it is quite another to open one's mouth and verify it." "Whoso keepeth his mouth and his tongue keepeth his soul from troubles."— Proverbs 21:23.

✦✦✦✦✦✦✦✦✦✦✦

Look at verses 6, 7, 8, 13, 19, 21. Verse 24 is profound wisdom concerning friendship. Compare this with Proverbs 17:17.

What's In A Name?

Proverbs 22

"Blind, senseless brutality! No conscience! No sense of right or wrong! Violence for the sake of violence! This is the frightening face of juvenile crime in its most terrible form." J. Edgar Hoover in *This Week* magazine, October 26, 1958. "Unless this tide of evil is checked," he goes on to say, "by 1962 there will be a million teen-age criminals in the United States."

Like cool water in suffocating heat is the admonition concerning discipline in the home which is sprinkled throughout the proverbs. From the innocent-seeming indulgence and over-protection of the father who doesn't want his son to "go through what I went through," to the extreme case of the father who just doesn't care and therefore abdicates and gives the child anything he wants rather than be bothered, the results are the same. Children grow up with a general indifference to authority and responsibility and for them home is more like a "country club."

And the pay-off—a generation of youngsters whose standard of being adult is to "do as I please." Never more than today does the American home need the strong medicine of Proverbs 22:6 and 15. The good name of some families would suffer less, if this counsel were taken more seriously. "For whom the Lord loveth He correcteth; even as a father the son in whom he delighteth."—Proverbs 3:12.

****

Can the responsibility of the parent be delegated? Give some thought to the criteria by which boys judge themselves to be men. What is "manly" in their eyes? What are the things boys do to be "grown up?" Where do these ideas of manliness come from?

Never Underestimate The Power Of A Woman

Proverbs 31

These proverbs may seem a bit old fashioned to the modern man, nevertheless, one finds it impossible to avoid nostalgia as he reads about the good woman described in this chapter. The Book of Proverbs has plenty to say about the evil woman whose devices bring destruction to the young man as well as to his loved ones. Proverbs 31 portrays the opposite, a good woman, whose influence is immeasurable and never to be forgotten.

Dr. Andrew W. Blackwood, a favorite professor in seminary, used to remind his classes from time to time of the inestimable value of a good woman in the life of a man, and conversely, the potentially devastating influence of an evil woman. To do this he used a formula which is interesting to contemplate.

> A good woman has the power to make a bad man good,

THE POWER OF A WOMAN

A bad woman has the power to make a good man bad.

Rarely does a good man have the power to make a bad woman good,

Or a bad man have the power to make a good woman bad.

The balance of power is with the woman. She may be thought of as the weaker sex, but God has built into womanhood a strength which no man enjoys and without which no man can be everything he ought to be.

How long has it been since you told your wife you loved her? How long since you gave her any evidence whatever of your love? You say, "She knows I love her." Sure she does, but she likes to hear you say it just the same. You've been so busy being a good husband, bringing home the bacon, etc., that you haven't had time to give your beloved wife the attention every good woman needs. At least you can let her know how much she means to you. It will do a great deal for a faithful woman to be told by her loved ones what her life means to them. Don't wait until Mother's day, do it now. "My son, keep thy father's commandment, and forsake not the law of thy mother; bind them continually upon thine heart, and tie them about thy neck. When thou goest, it shall lead thee; when thou sleepest, it shall keep thee; and when thou wakest, it shall talk with thee."—Proverbs 6:20-22.

❋❋❋❋❋❋❋❋❋❋❋❋

It would not be amiss to indulge a few moments in thinking over the influence of a Godly mother or wife or sister or sweetheart, a consideration which hardheaded businessmen are apt to neglect for fear of what they call sentimentalism.

New Testament Capitalism

Matthew 25:14-30

Matthew 25 consists of a series of parables by which Jesus teaches the nature of His kingdom. The passage for our consideration gives a picture of one phase of Christian stewardship, the stewardship of possessions. It is difficult to see how anyone taking the Bible seriously can use it to justify the doctrine of socialism. The Ten Commandments clearly teach the sanctity of property rights. "Thou shalt not steal, thou shalt not covet . . ." The Bible teaches the right and the obligation of private ownership and private enterprise.

This matter of obligation is the point at which capitalism or any system breaks down. With every privilege there is a corresponding responsibility and one forsakes the privilege if he rejects the responsibility. Irresponsible men, who abuse their right of possession, are not an argument against capitalism, (such men would exploit socialism or any other system selfishly) they simply confirm the fact that human nature itself tends to be greedy, selfish, covetous, envious, for which reason its redemption by Jesus Christ is imperative.

The Christian view of so-called capitalism is summed up in the word "stewardship." Stewardship begins with the conviction that life is a trust from God, that everything we are and everything we have is from Him originally. He is the giver "of every good and perfect gift." "A man can receive nothing, except it be given him from heaven." Stewardship teaches that man owns nothing ("Naked came I into the world . . ."), that all he possesses belongs to God Who holds the right of eminent domain. Man therefore is accountable to God as to the use he makes of the gift of life itself and all its benefits.

A good steward (which is a way of saying a true Christian) is one who sees life as a trust from God and is therefore determined to buy up every opportunity so that life will be fully productive and God will be glorified. He does not bury his talent for fear of losing it, he invests his talent so that it may bring a return and he will have more to offer his Lord when he stands before him to "give an account of the deeds done in the flesh." He does not just want to vegetate during his lifetime, he wants to live, to labor, to love, to make life count for God.

Notice that those who received talents were required to put those talents to work. They were expected to invest them in order that they might earn while the master was absent. The sin of the one-talent man was that he failed to put his talent to use. The judgment for such negligence is clear, his talent was taken from him. If you fail to use what God has given, you lose it in the final analysis. Bury it for the sake of keeping it and you lose it.

Talent must be invested to be kept, that is life. Of course, risk is involved—you have to let it go in order to get it back again with increase. He that saves his life loses, he that loses his life for Christ's sake, finds it. "Except a grain of wheat fall into the ground and die, it abideth alone . . ." A million dollars is worthless while it is buried. In itself it is nothing, its value is what it will buy. Thus the miser loses everything. And so does the spiritual miser!

Incidentally, the accidents and catastrophes of life often force men to re-evaluate life quickly, and in the process, the transposition of values is sometimes very interesting. As the Titanic was sinking, men were trying desperately to trade diamond bracelets and brooches, pearl necklaces and earrings for an orange or two. With life and death the clear issue, priceless jewelry was so much bauble. Probably a jewel thief under such circumstances would become an orange thief, although some men are so blind that the jewelry would come first. It did in fact, with some, and they sank to an icy, watery grave clutching their property.

Here are taught the two important phases of stewardship, production or use, and accountability. God builds into me certain talents which become part of the life He gives me at birth and places me in a world full of the raw materials with which to make life fruitful. With the talents God put in me, I take the raw materials which He gives to make them produce to His glory. *The man, who does not recognize God's right to the fruit of his toil, has not begun to enjoy life!* "For who maketh thee to differ from another, and what hast thou that thou didst not receive? Now if thou didst receive it, why dost thou glory, as if thou hadst not received it."—1 Corinthians 4:7.

❧❧❧❧❧❧❧❧❧❧❧❧

Look up Luke 6:38. Here is stated the reward of faithful stewardship. Someone has said, "You cannot outgive God." How true! God will be no man's debtor. The man who neglects to invest in the work of Christ and His Kingdom in the world is only robbing himself ultimately. In this context, you will be interested in studying Malachi 3:8-10.

The Inevitable Out-
come Of Secularism

Matthew 21:33-41

Secularism seems so innocent and harmless on the surface. After all so many good people are secular-minded—they seem to take no interest in spiritual things. They never harm anybody, tend to their own business, have a good time, work hard—why not let them be? The trouble is that man is a social being and secularism in collective man is like a contagious disease that spreads rapidly when not isolated. Putting two secular men together does not just mean twice as much secularism, but a hundred times as much. You're not dealing with integers, you're dealing with a malignancy, the infectious cells of which are explosive. For this reason a man will do things in a crowd he would never think of doing alone. This is the reason a vocal few can sometimes stir a crowd into hysteria and make it do things which those who make up the crowd will regret for a long time.

159

Isolate one secular man and you find much in him to admire perhaps. But see secularism for what it is, a disease which may turn into an epidemic out of control, and you appreciate how destructive, how anti-Godless it is potentially. Actually, secularism is worse than communism for secularism is the soil from which communism and systems like it spring. Secularism is the root, Communism is one of the fruits. In Communism we see one of the worst forms of secularism, but before the rise of Communism, secularism produced other systems and history records the devastation which these infected systems wrought on the world.

Actually, secularism is a false religion, the father of all false religions. It is the religion of materialism, its god is things. The religion of things invariably crucifies the Son of God, which is the point of this parable. Through the centuries men have killed or stoned or beaten or disregarded and humiliated the prophets of God. Finally, God sent His Son, and they crucified Him.

Materialism has been crucifying Jesus Christ generation by generation for the past 1900 years. It has been said of Americans that "we love things and use people." If this be true, even partially, what an indictment of a nation that is supposed to be grounded on spiritual foundations. Wise is the man who has learned to keep a clear line between his life and his possessions. Foolish the man who is deceived into thinking that life equals possessions. When a man makes money, or any possession his idol, he turns his back on God and walks away from Jesus Christ to his own eternal shame and doom. "No man can serve two masters; for either he will hate the one and love the other; or else he will hold to the one and despise the other. Ye cannot serve God and mammon."—Matthew 6:24.

❖❖❖❖❖❖❖❖❖❖❖

In this setting it will be profitable to distinguish between riches and the love of riches. There are those who teach against riches, as though poverty is a virtue and riches an evil. The Bible does not hold this to be true. Often poor people love money more than wealthy people. It is not what a man has but his attitude toward what he has.

The Spirit Of Giving

2 Corinthians 9:6-15

Quality, not quantity counts in giving. God is interested in the spirit of the giver, not in the size of the gift. This is fundamental to Christian stewardship in the matter of offerings. God is not in need of money! "The cattle on a thousand hills" belong to Him, "the silver and the gold" are His. He is the "giver of every good and perfect gift." It is unmitigated impertinence to speak as if the work of the Lord were in desperate need of man's money. This attitude is probably one reason why some Christian activity suffers perennial financial difficulty. Instead of looking to God to supply their need, they look to men, as though they were the source of supply. Man is only the channel, God is the source. Better not to allow a man to give who is not moved by the Spirit of God so to do than to receive his gift and alienate him.

God is not on the verge of bankruptcy, ever!

God does not receive man's offering because He needs a gift, but because man needs to give! Man is at his best when giving. His manliness suffers if he will not give. Personality is always warped in the one who will not give or who gives in the wrong spirit. (Remember Scrooge?) Man has missed the greatest blessing if he has not learned to give God's way. He is something less than a man who is not a Christian steward. In His providence, God has condescended to allow man to share in His eternal enterprise. This is life's highest privilege!

No man owns what he has, God owns it! Man possesses it, but it is God's. Man is the trustee for forty or fifty or sixty years, and he fulfills his highest role in life when he handles his possessions as a trust from God. He is most manly, most dependable, most productive, whose trusteeship is handled with a due awareness of his accountability to God.

This is the economics of the kingdom of God: God gives man the capital, lets him invest it back into kingdom business, enjoy the fellowship of participation in His eternal purpose, and reap eternal dividends with interest compounded eternally. This is what is meant by "laying up treasure in heaven."

Someone has said, "You can't take it with you, but you can send it on ahead." Get it out of your head that God needs your money. Don't give anything if your giving is on that basis! Keep your money to yourself. Money given grudgingly blesses neither giver nor receiver.

Paul suggests three principles of Christian giving: it should be done systematically, a man should "purpose in his heart" what he will give. This is planned giving, not haphazard, hit or miss giving. Christian giving should be done cheerfully, not of necessity, for "God loves a cheerful giver." And giving should be as unto the Lord. Give your gift as though you were putting it into the nail-scarred hands of Jesus Christ. Whatever the use to which your gift is being put, give it as unto the Lord. "Not because I desire a gift, but I desire fruit that may abound to your account."—Philippians 4:17.

❖❖❖❖❖❖❖❖❖❖❖

It is not accidental that the eighth verse which contains one of the most fantastic promises in the Bible is given in the context of Christian giving. The life principle of stewardship is found in verse 6, its logic is irresistible. Think it through!

The Most Important Quality In Stewardship

1 Corinthians 4:1-7

If you needed someone to handle your affairs with as much interest as you yourself would take, what would you look for in the men you interviewed for the job? What attribute above all others would commend a prospect to you?

The biblical word "stewardship" describes one who has such heavy responsibility, a trusted representative who is expected to manage the affairs as well as or better than the owner himself. The steward was in charge when the master was absent. All lines of responsibility flowed to him and he reported directly to the owner.

Of all the qualities befitting the steward, Paul the Apostle mentions "faithfulness" as being the one required. If the steward is faithful or trustworthy, one need not be too concerned about other qualities, and conversely, if he is not faithful, whatever other attributes he possesses, he could not be entrusted with such responsibility. In fact, the better equipped the man is who is not faithful, the less he is to be trusted. The clever bad man is more dangerous than the stupid one.

Faithfulness comprehends many other qualities important to a man in the place of trust. It implies loyalty or allegiance. The steward is aware that all he possesses comes from the master and belongs to him. He has, therefore, a sense of accountability to the master which includes the willingness to reserve judgment until all the facts are in and the master himself judges (verses 3-5). The steward cares for the master's possessions as though they were his own.

Faithfulness implies stick-to-itiveness or follow through. The faithful steward is a good finisher. He takes things as they come, good or bad, pleasant or unpleasant, having no freedom to forsake his post, however difficult. "Do not be deceived, my beloved brethren, every good endowment and every perfect gift is from above, coming down from the Father of lights with whom there is no variation or shadow due to change."—James 1:16-17 (R.S.V.)

❖❖❖❖❖❖❖❖❖❖❖

Verse 7 of the passage under consideration is

good material for the so-called "self-made man" to contemplate. The worst arrogance of which man is capable is that which overlooks the fact that God Himself is the source of all life and energy and strength and ability. The really good man is humble in the light of this recognition. The best you can say about the "self-made man" is that it's good of him not to blame anyone else.

Have You Ever Been An Answer To Prayer?

2 Corinthians 1:3-7

The answering side of prayer is as important as the asking side! We make a lot of the *praying man*, but do we overlook what is equally important, that is the *answering man?* Has it ever occurred to you that God might want to use you this way? It is possible that you are God's answer to somebody else's prayer.

One three-star Marine General, now retired, at one time the ranking officer of the Corps, when he was Commanding Officer of the largest Marine training base, went out of his way to encourage recruits. He figured their mothers were praying for them, and he wanted to do what he could to honor those prayers. This tough fighting man, who went through plenty of hell in the Pacific during World War II, says he probably doesn't pray as much as he should, but he has always been concerned for the men under his command. He knows how mothers pray for their sons in battle.

George Mueller is known for his amazing prayers. He prayed literally millions of dollars into orphanage support. There was nothing phony about it, as attested by one hard and fast rule which Mueller never violated. This practice confirms the authenticity of Mueller's praying: He believed in influencing men through prayer to God alone. When there was a need, Mueller told God, never man.

But just as amazing is the fact that whenever Mueller prayed, God had a man somewhere, sensitive to His will, who would respond to the impulse of the Holy Spirit and answer Mueller's prayer. Mueller's faith was tremendous, but the faithfulness of the men God used to match that faith was equally remarkable!

Look at it this way. Maybe someone's prayers remain unanswered because the man God wants to use to answer it is unavailable or disobedient. Insensitive to God's leading, a man may hinder prayer, not just his own, but other's as well. The man out of touch with God may hinder another man's blessing. Being out of fellowship with God always works a double evil—not only the man himself suffers, but those whom God intends to benefit through his obedience. "... the God of all comfort, who comforts us, so that we may be able to comfort those who are in affliction, with the comfort with which we ourselves are comforted by God."—2 Corinthians 1:4.

❖❖❖❖❖❖❖❖❖❖❖

The continuity is interesting here. Not only does one man's disobedience affect another, but his affliction also. The comfort he receives from the Lord becomes that which he comforts another. Are you in the place where God can use you to answer another man's prayer?

CHAPTER

SIX

Man Of Influence

Pardon, Your Character Is Showing

Romans 15:1-7

It is indisputable that a man's witness for Christ begins with what he is rather than what he says. He may talk until he is "blue in the face" and leave people unimpressed if his life does not add up. *A Christian's performance either verifies or contradicts his profession.* What he is determines whether or not men will take seriously what he says.

Our twentieth century society is conditioned to performance. Without it, they remain unsold. They have a right to expect a Christian to act like a Christian. They cannot be expected to be impressed with Christian faith if they do not see in Christians something more than they see in themselves or others who have no faith.

The reputation of Jesus Christ rides on the consistency of Christians to many outside the Church. Every Christian's testimony would carry more weight if he lived as though he had to earn the right to be heard. Of course this places a burden on the Christian, a burden which some in the Church are not willing to assume and whose lives therefore are a reproach to Christ. Their witness for Christ is a caricature, a misrepresentation, a distortion of what a Christian is, and their lives repel men from Christ and His Church.

The irony is that it is more difficult to be a half-hearted Christian than a completely dedicated one. It's always the fence-rider whose life is in precarious balance, who walks like a man on a tight rope. He is constantly vacillating between the appeal of a thoroughly Christian life and the deadening drag of compromise and sub-Christian living. He never really enjoys either. He is like a man riding two horses that are running off in opposite directions. The strain is terrible.

Whereas, the man who goes all the way with Christ and is determined that his life will be a credit to the Church, finds that God has made available all the resources any man needs to live an effective and attractive life. The standards are high, but the resources of God, whereby those standards are achievable, are present and available. "And God is able to make all grace abound toward you, that you, always having all sufficiency in all things, may abound unto every good work."—2 Corinthians 9:8.

❧❧❧❧❧❧❧❧❧❧❧❧

The heart of this admonition in Romans 15:1-7 has to do with one's relationship with others. The principle is three-fold: The strong must bear the infirmities of the weak, a Christian should not live to please himself but to please his neighbor, and he should live in harmony with all men.

Guide To Christian Conduct

1 Corinthians 10:23-31

According to the Apostle Paul, the Christian is "not under the law . . ." "All things are lawful for me . . ." This does not mean that the Christian is lawless, but it does mean that he is ruled by something higher than law. He is subject to Divine grace. This makes sense. Law is for the lawless, not for the law-abiding. A man does not refrain from murder simply because there is a statute against it. You would not murder even if there were no law forbidding it. You were born with a built-in conscience which has far greater force than outward ordinances to keep you in line.

So the Christian is governed, not by moral, ethical and religious statutes, although the Bible sets these forth as a guide and norm, but by the presence of Christ within. He has more than conscience, he has the Spirit of God, Who literally dwells in him and who makes him sensitive to the pleasure of God and gives him the desire and delight to do the will of God.

In 1 Corinthians 10:23-31, five principles are listed as guides to conduct. From the lowest to the highest, they are: expediency, edification, another's wealth (or interests), another's conscience, and the glory of God. The highest standard for the Christian is to do everything he does, even eating and drinking, to the glory of God. The Shorter Catechism of the Presbyterian and Reformed tradition begins with an illuminating question: "What is the chief end of man?" The answer, "Man's chief end is to glorify God and to enjoy him forever."

❖❖❖❖❖❖❖❖❖❖❖❖

Does a Christian have a right to do as he pleases because he is not under the law? For your own edification, try to see how each of the principles set forth in the text would apply to specific situations in your experience.

The Key To Human Relations

1 John 1:1-10

Life in its simplest terms is right relationship. Domestic tranquility is assured when the relations between husband and wife, child with parent and child with child are what they should be. Industrial harmony depends upon the management-labor relationship. Everything suffers when human relations fail. The breakdown of society, regardless of the level, is due fundamentally to a breakdown in human relations.

Not to be overlooked is the fact that human relations are hierarchal. To illustrate, in the home the relation between parent and child is more important than child with child. In industry, the relation between management and labor is more important than labor with labor. In fact, it is possible to have children in a home rightly related to each other but insubordinate to their parents. When children gang up on parents, anarchy prevails and the home suffers.

177

By the same token, important as are the relations of the laboring man to his fellow laborers, even more important is the relationship between labor and management.

Basic to all of life's relationships is that between man and God. When this is right, all others are bound to be right. Christianity begins with reconciliation between God and man and this is reflected in man's relation with his fellowman. (See 2 Corinthians 5:19)

At the heart of the breakdown of all human relations is sin. Sin separates: Man from God, man from man, husband from wife, child from parent, management from labor, etc. Sin even divides a man himself, making him do what he hates and fail to do what he likes. The damage resulting from sin is incalculable: Man hours lost. Homes broken. Mental illness. Suicides. Skidrow wrecks. Sin is the disease that produces them all! Man's solutions fail because they deal with the symptoms, *Christianity works because it deals with the disease.*

In the passage being considered, the Apostle John makes much of fellowship. This is the highest form of human relationship because it has God at the center (verse 3). Verses 5 and 6 lay bare the bottom problem in fellowship. What destroys fellowship is unconfessed sin. The man who refuses to admit his sin, who will not confess to God and apologize to man when proper, brings a rift into fellowship. He can neither walk with God or his fellowman. It is not too difficult to recall someone in your experience (perhaps yourself) who because of stubborn pride, brought a cleavage between himself and a friend and loved one. The rift persisted and deepened and broadened until apologies had been made and reconciliation took place. This is what John is talking about in verses 5-9. These few verses contain the profoundest truth in the matter of protecting and preserving right relations between all men. "Love God with all your heart . . . and your neighbor as yourself."

�֍✤✤✤✤✤✤✤✤✤

How would you define fellowship? What is the important thing about the fellowship John discusses? Notice John's statement of purpose in verse 4.

Christianity In The Home

Ephesians 5:21—6:4

We accept the fact that the home is the basic unit in society. We know that no nation can long survive its demoralization and degeneration. Even Russian Communism was forced to recognize the importance of maintaining the integrity of the home. Yet it is possible to go along academically with these self-evident truths, and actually fail to maintain a truly Christian home life.

You've perhaps heard the story of the man who claimed in a testimony meeting to have become sinlessly perfect, at which his pastor countered, "We'll check with your wife and children about this."

Contemplate the prospect if every father took as his first responsibility the Christianizing of his own home. This task cannot be delegated to the Church or to the school. If the father fails, the home has desperately slim chances of being what it should be. The father's responsibility cannot be evaded. Where it is accepted, the home becomes a Church, a school, and a blessing to all within its borders and its community.

In verse 21 the Apostle Paul sets down the general principle governing all human relationships, the principle of submission to each other in the Lord. Following he gives the application of this for the wives, verses 22-24, husbands, verses 25-31, children, verses 6:1-3, parents, verse 6:4.

The standard of a wife's relationship with her husband is that of the Church to Christ. As the Church is subject to Christ her Lord, so the wife should be to her own husband in everything. But this submission is not meant as slavish subservience to a domineering man, for the same principle is binding upon him. The husband is to love his wife as Christ loved His Church—and laid down His life for her. The husband's love for his wife must be a sacrificial love. No wife need fear submission to a man who loves her as Christ loved His Church. "And the Lord God said, it is not good that the man should be alone; I will make him a help meet for him."—Genesis 2:18.

❉❉❉❉❉❉❉❉❉❉❉❉

How does the analogy of the Church fit into this picture? What is your reaction to the idea that the child gets his idea of the Fatherhood of God from his own father in the home? Does this passage contain any hint as to the way of reconciliation in a home where there is serious alienation? Please note that the submission of the wife is voluntary, not mandatory. Jesus Christ never "makes" the Church submit to Him. Christ is not a tyrant!

Husbands, Love Your Wives

Ephesians 5:25-31

"It's a pity to go to another man when these things should be discussed with my husband . . ." Thus spoke a wife who was at the end of the line! For ten years she had endured life with a man who, though decent and honorable and successful, never allowed a subject vital to his marriage to be opened for discussion. He laid down the law, and the matter was closed. He simply refused to converse.

His friends thought he was the greatest. "They think he is an angel," she said, "and he is to his friends . . . I'd much rather have him for a friend than a husband!" She had waited ten years to confide in a counsellor and still she was humiliated and ashamed that she had to discuss these intimacies with an outsider. But she had to talk to somebody! Her grievances had been bottled up too long and now they were exploding. She couldn't sit on the lid any longer.

How do you figure the man who will let a gulf widen in his marriage? He knows the importance of communication in business and will pay high prices for advertisers who can tell the story. He is constantly working to improve his own communication technique. Public relations are essential to his business. Yet he totally ignores the desperately important lines of communication at home. His wife is dying to talk through the deeper things of their marriage with him, yet she is never able to win a hearing.

"Those rare moments are sheer golden when my husband takes time to talk with me," said one young woman whose hardworking husband was always too busy or too weary. Being practical, he figured he paid the bills, gave the wife plenty to live on, didn't drink too much, didn't run around with other women, worked hard—what more does she want? She wants into his life, a little share at least. She wants to let him into her life, share herself with her beloved. She just wants *him!*

No marriage can endure silence! The wife may grit her teeth, hang on by sheer strength of will, but love dies. The marriage may stay together, but it's on the rocks as surely as if divorce were final. "Husbands, love your wives as Christ loved the Church and gave Himself for her . . ."—Ephesians 5:25.

❖❖❖❖❖❖❖❖❖❖❖

HUSBANDS, LOVE YOUR WIVES

It is said that one of the most common difficulties in the modern home is the lack of conversation between husband and wife. Mornings, at the breakfast table, he's buried in the newspaper, evenings after dinner, everybody's looking at T.V. Rarely if ever do husbands and wives have an opportunity to talk things through together unless they make time for it. The standard of a husband's love for his wife is the highest standard there is, the love of Christ for His Church. Jesus said, "Greater love hath no man than this, that he lay down his life for his friends." That is the kind of love the Christian husband is expected to have for his wife.

Christianity In Industry

Ephesians 6:5-9

Christian responsibility is a two-way road. Whether it is in the home or on the job, every privilege is accompanied by corresponding responsibility. The husband has a right to expect certain things from his wife, but let him not neglect his obligation as a husband. The father may demand certain conduct from his children, but he has a holy obligation to them. The employer has the right to the time and productive capacity of his employee, but this involves Christian responsibility on his part. To neglect the responsibility is to repudiate the privilege.

The Christian employee is required by the Bible to be obedient to his employer and to put the interests of the employer first during the working hours. In this obligation, he is to do it, not simply as unto the "boss" but as one who pleases God. The Christian employee must remember that he honors God by faithfulness on the job. This is his duty as a servant of Christ. Doing anything less than his best is unworthy.

The employer who is Christian treats his employees as a servant of the Lord remembering that he himself has an obligation to God, that both he and his employee serve the same Master.

It becomes apparent as one reads the New Testament that Christianity involves and enhances all of life, it is not simply a department of life effective Sunday morning only. The Christian who sees no connection between his faith and his business has failed to comprehend the meaning of his faith. "It is required of stewards that a man be found faithful." —1 Corinthians 4:2.

❖❖❖❖❖❖❖❖❖❖❖

According to the Christian standard, where does the balance of power lie in industrial relations? What is the guiding Christian principle in all industrial relations?

Christianity In The Church

Romans 14:1-13

A great Danish theologian was led into disillusionment as a boy when he observed the glaring inconsistencies in the lives of the members of his Church. He found it impossible to understand a piety that seemed to take God seriously in the sanctuary on Sunday and then live as though there were no God the balance of the week. He asked himself a very penetrating question, "How do you make Christians out of people who are already Christian?"

What does it take to get Christians to act like Christians? That is the big question! Perhaps one of the reasons those outside the Church take Christianity "with a grain of salt," is because they see so little authentic Christianity in the Church. It was said of the Apostolic Church that it "had favor with all the people." (Acts 2:47) That does not mean that the Church was popular necessarily, but it does mean that whatever the outsider felt about their religion, the consistency of their lives could not be gainsaid. Their Godliness was a credit to their Lord and their Church.

"Lo, how they love one another," was also said of that primitive Church. Love for the brethren is the hallmark of genuine Christianity. In the Scripture under consideration, it is important to note that the one who thinks himself strong in the faith increases his responsibility to love and understand the brother who is weak. The very fact a man feels he is in a position to criticize a brother, places upon him the burden of loving and supporting the brother. Criticism that flows from any other spirit is simply the projection of the critic's own weakness, and evidence of his pale and transparent attempt to cover up for himself.

The test as to whether one's insight about a brother is spiritual or not, is whether he prays for that brother or criticizes him. The insight which the Spirit of God gives concerning another leads inevitably to prayer. *Insight that provokes criticism does not have its origin in the Spirit.* Discernment that comes from God burdens you to talk to God about the person. If you find yourself talking to others about him, your discernment is certainly not from God. ". . . If I have not love, I have nothing. . . Love does not insist on its own way; it is not irritable or resentful; it does not rejoice at wrong, but rejoices in the right. Love bears all things. . ."—1 Corinthians 13 (R.S.V.)

✿✿✿✿✿✿✿✿✿✿✿

What will be the attitude of a mature Christian to one who is new in the faith? To one weak in the faith?

Your Real Influence

Galatians 5:16-24

Unconscious influence is what counts in the long run. It's a man's real influence. Not what he says when he carefully chooses his words or what he does when he tries consciously to impress someone. It is not what he is when he is working to make a point or when he has himself under control, but what he is when he's not trying, when he's relaxed—what a man is apart from effort, the real self keeps coming through to people all the time, comes through what he says, what he does and what he tries to be. And this unconscious influence either confirms or contradicts the impression he is trying to make.

It boils down to this, that a man cannot control his real influence. It flows from within him, from deep down underneath his consciousness. Like an iceberg, six-sevenths of a man is below the surface, and this uncontrollable six-sevenths asserts itself constantly.

Many a boy has been scarred for life by an influence in his father of which the father was totally unaware. The boy's character was molded and his destiny jelled in terms of an example in his father over which the father had no control.

For this reason too, Christianity has the practical answer. Because it goes to work at the center of man's being where it really matters. Jesus told His disciples that it was to their advantage that He returned to His heavenly Father following the resurrection. "When I go," He said, "I will send the Comforter" (The Counsellor) Who is the Holy Spirit, and "He will be in you."

God, by His Spirit actually indwells the Christian, and working within, produces bonafide Christian character, making a man's unconscious influence a Christ-like influence. True Christianity is not trying to be something a man cannot be, it is literally letting Christ, by the Spirit, be himself in all of life.

Quit trying to be what you can't! Admit your need and submit to Christ. This is authentic Christian influence, recognizing his own sin and inadequacy, the Christian turns the controls of his life over to Christ. *Christ, reigning from within, controls the uncontrollable.* Jesus said, "He who abides in Me, and I in him, he it is that bears much fruit, for apart from me you can do nothing."—John 15:5.

YOUR REAL INFLUENCE

There is a sense in which Christian virtue is effortless, like the emergence of fruit on a branch (Galatians 5:22). The bankruptcy of the flesh is evident in Galatians 5:19-21. Even at its best the flesh cannot hide that which is native to it. Christian character is fruit bearing by the power of the Holy Spirit and the condition for such bearing is simple. See Galatians 5:16.

Wait Till The Facts Are In

Genesis 45:4-8

Don't be to quick to judge results! It has been said that the only exercise some men get is jumping at conclusions. This habit is quite common among Christians. They get all upset with things as they are because they evaluate in the midst of the process instead of waiting to see the outcome. Joseph was probably discouraged often and wondered why life was playing him such dirty tricks. But he sweat out the injustice and meanness of his brothers and Pharoah's court and discovered that God used evil circumstances to raise him to the highest position in the land. What the brothers meant for evil, God meant for good.

That's an amazing thing about God! He can take the worst that man can do to you and turn it into the best thing that ever happened. The clue to perseverance is to remind oneself of the absolute justice and faithfulness of God. Circumstances may look bad but never allow them to undermine the character of God and rob you of confidence in Him. Stay on God's side—come what may, you'll never regret it. "They that wait on the Lord shall inherit the earth."—Psalm 37:9.

❊❊❊❊❊❊❊❊❊❊❊

You may not see the end from the beginning, but God does! You don't insist on seeing the destination before you begin a journey—you just take it as it comes mile by mile and you make it. God is leading, make no mistake on that . . . unless you don't want Him to . . . and He'll get you there, in good shape.

CHAPTER SEVEN

Man Of The World

The Church, A Lay-Movement

Ephesians 4:8m 11-16

A man will never understand the Church until he sees it as a lay movement. Whenever the layman becomes inactive in the work of the ministry, leaving it to the clergy, the Church declines. The Apostolic Church was a lay movement. When Jesus selected His disciples, He did not choose youth who had not yet settled on a vocation or career, He chose men for whom life had jelled, hardened men, veterans of a vocation in which they had already won their spurs. He chose fishermen and tax collectors.

On the day of Pentecost, 120 disciples were gathered in the upper room. Whatever happened that day, happened to everyone of them. The record says that Jews gathered in Jerusalem from "every nation under heaven" and each heard the Gospel in his own tongue because of the witness of the 120. These 120 were not "professionals," They were not clergymen with a degree in theology. They were "run-of-the-mill" men and women like you meet every day in your business. They were business men, artisans, laborers, housewives, teachers, etc.

Subsequently, persecution set in at Jerusalem causing the Church to be dispersed, all except the apostles, and those who were scattered by persecution "went everywhere preaching the Gospel." These scattered ones were laymen. The first martyr, Stephen, was a layman. The first evangelist, Philip, was a layman. Paul himself, the great apostle, who wrote half of the New Testament, had a vocation by which he made his living.

And Paul makes it very clear in his letter to the Ephesians that the work of the ministry rests squarely upon the shoulders of every Christian, no exceptions. The gifts Christ gave to some were in order that they might equip the whole Church to do the work of the ministry. The Great Commission was not committed to a relatively few "professionals" but to the whole Church. The work of the ministry belongs to the man in the pew and it will never be done any other way. "That which we have seen and heard declare we unto you, that you also may have fellowship with us. . ."

❧❧❧❧❧❧❧❧❧❧❧❧

Read Ephesians Chapter four from the beginning and see how Paul indicates that every individual Christian has a part in the ministry of the Church, for each of us is a member of a living organism which needs all its parts to fulfill its task in the world.

Has Christianity Failed?

Here is the familiar "Christmas story" of the birth of Jesus. Our interest is especially centered in verse 14. There are those who repudiate Christianity on the basis of this verse. They say Christianity is irrelevant and holds out no real hope for the world in its struggle, pointing to this verse as evidence. Here is a promise of peace, made 1900 years ago, yet how little peace the earth has enjoyed since the promise was made. So the reasoning goes. How do you explain the disparity between this remarkable, hopeful declaration and the facts as they are?

The answer to this query brings us to the heart of the human problem. A slight variation in the translation (consistent with the original language) will illustrate the point. One translator puts it this way; ". . . and on earth peace among men of good will." The Revised Standard Version translates it this way; ". . . and on earth peace among men with whom God is pleased." This puts the emphasis in the right place. Not peace, good will among men who are unwilling to have peace God's way, but peace among men whose wills are right toward God's way of peace. God's peace is available—on God's conditions, obviously! *God's peace is for men of good will.* It works when men's wills are right. In the fundamental sense, sin springs from man's will. Sin is revolt—man's revolt against God's order. Man's will is bad toward God. This rebellion expresses itself in man's desire to have things his own way. Man is a rebel in God's world and before peace can prevail, man must cease his rebellion.

"All we like sheep have gone astray, we have turned everyone to his own way. . ."—Isaiah 53:6. "Everyone to his own way . . ." This is sin. Men of good will are men who turn from their own way to God's. Men of good will are men who are willing to obey God (John 7:17). In other words, *Christianity works when men work it.* Christianity has not failed . . . men have failed to work it!

❖❖❖❖❖❖❖❖❖❖❖❖

What do we mean when we say "secularism?" What are its symptoms? What is dangerous about it? Does it have anything to do with man's indifference to God? Does it have anything to do with the rift among men and nations? Does it have anything to do with war? What is the difference between anarchy (spiritually speaking) and secularism? Does the will of man have anything to do with secular spirit?

Authentic Christian Influence

Acts 8:1-8

Talk about infiltration! Communism cannot hold a candle to Christ's witnesses around the world. Christ has His men everywhere. The real impact of the Church is not a huge religious combine or power bloc, overpowering by sheer force of numbers. It is not a massive show of solidarity or institutional might. The power of Christ's Church is infinitely more subtle, infinitely more effective.

Man's intelligence and counter-intelligence work is infinitesimal compared to God's infusion of Christians into all life everywhere. The Divine strategy is the Christian man, at his job day in day out, bearing witness to Christ by life and lip right where he lives and works and plays. In business and industry, government and the professions, labor, education, the military, in strategic places around the world—behind the iron curtain, probably right in the Kremlin and Peking (He had men in Caesar's houshold in Paul's day), Christ has His witnesses.

This spiritual penetration is the clue to the incredible, incalculable influence of Christianity worldwide. The teacher doing his job to the glory of God, the student witnessing for Christ on the campus, in the fraternity house or dormitory, on the football field or in the student lounge. The Christian labor leader, businessman, military officer, policeman, surgeon, dentist, architect, merchant, housewife, farmer, lawyer, in Congress and parliaments, in the Pentagon and the State Department, in banks and clubs and lodges, in coal mines and steel mills—by the tens of thousands, by the millions, working, living for Christ. This is the real picture of authentic Christian influence. This is the Church rightly understood. This is invincible Christianity against which the gates of hell shall not prevail.

"But you shall receive power when the Holy Spirit has come upon you; and you shall be my witnesses in Jerusalem and in all Judea and Samaria and to the end of the earth."—Acts 1:8.

✸✸✸✸✸✸✸✸✸✸✸

It isn't what happens on Sunday morning in the sanctuary that is the measure of the influence of the Church, but what happens when the sanctuary is deserted, what happens Monday through Saturday in your home, office, on your job, in your social set. You are the Church and it is your influence that is counting for or against Christ. Notice that every Christian in that primitive Church was scattered, and everyone of them preached the Gospel wherever he went. What was the *one* condition to be a witness?

The Deception In Foreign Missions

Luke 24:45-53

There is a subtle danger in the designation FOR-EIGN missions! It is that one limits the mission of the Church to the other side of the ocean. Which of course is utterly contrary to the truth as it is in the Bible.

Actually the mission of the Church begins right outside its doors. Wherever there is a man or woman or child unevangelized, there is the mission of the Church. Jesus mildly rebuked his disciples on one occasion with words which awakened them to this fact, "Say not there are yet four months and then cometh the harvest. Lift up your eyes unto the fields already white unto harvest." Just look around you, that's where the mission of the Church begins!

One of the common ailments of the American Christian is this paradoxical excitement over the salvation of a head-hunter in Formosa or a pygmy in Africa or an Indian in the hinterland of Brazil, meanwhile ignoring the neighbor next door who is just as lost without Jesus Christ. And incidentally, this attitude gets its reaction on the part of the "natives." They find it difficult to understand why Americans feel so strongly the necessity of preaching exclusively to "foreigners" when there is much evidence of need right at home.

The acid test of one's genuine concern for the foreign mission of the Church is his concern for the friend next door. Surely the interest in the pagan half a world away is synthetic if there is no concern for the civilized pagan across the street. The whole mission of the Church is evangelism, the winning of the lost to Christ, and evangelism begins right where the Church is, right where the Christian is. One certainly will not be evangelistic where he is not, if he is not evangelistic where he is!

Wherever the Saviour moved during His earthly ministry, He was aware of the need about Him. "Seeing the multitudes, He had compassion on them." This was characteristic of Him, His sense of the need, the aloneness, the suffering, the despair, the sin and frustration of the crowds that pressed Him daily. This awareness of another's need, plus a prayerful concern to do something about it, is the true mission of the Church. And it begins right now, right where you are! "And that repentance and remission of sins should be preached in His name among all nations, *beginning at Jerusalem.*" —Luke 24:47.

****

Every true Christian should have the world on his heart! That is, he should be willing to settle for nothing less than evangelism world-wide. Not that everyone is to try to go everywhere doing everything for everybody, but that as each person does his job right where he is and prays that laborers are sent wherever God directs, each Christian's mission field will be the world and each will be following His call day in day out right where the Lord has placed Him. What is meant by "things" in verse 48?

Why Missions?

Romans 1:16-23

Often the question is asked, "Why do we preach to people of other nations who have their own religion? Is it not arrogant and presumptuous of us to try to get them to exchange their religion for ours?"

This is a good question and it has an adequate answer.

In the first place, it is incorrect to think of the goal of the missionary as being an attempt to get a "native" to exchange his religion for ours. Rightly understood, Christianity is infinitely more than religion. The message of the Christian missionary is the message of life eternal through Jesus Christ. Religion is man's effort to find God or placate an angry God for his sins. Christianity is the GOOD NEWS that God has come in Christ to forgive man's sins and offer him the gift of eternal life.

Remember that the religionists of Jesus' day represented His strongest opposition. They were incorrigibly hostile to Jesus and did not rest until they had liquidated Him. In the light of history, religion can mean most anything. It can be utterly Godless, as for example in the case of the Athenians (Acts 17). Religion can lead to the most inhuman practices such as infanticide, child brides, the burial alive of the wife or servants of the deceased, the worship of animals or fire or water, or anything man cannot understand, or control. It makes man bow down before the most grotesque inventions of his own hands. It has led to human sacrifice and the worst kind of human degradation.

Some of the wars and the most terrible atrocities that have scandalized history were perpetrated in the name of religion. The deplorable conditions under which some men live is due to their religion, not in spite of it.

But the mission of the Christian Church, when it is rightly understood, is not a matter of trying to get these people to scrap their religion for another. It is to get them to embrace the Gospel of Jesus Christ which has the power to redeem human nature from the terrible pit into which it has fallen. It is to tell them of the love of God in Christ and to urge them to receive God's loving provision for their eternal welfare.

The core of Christianity is not the ethics and doctrines of Christ but His death and resurrection. *The message of the missionary has to do with events, not ideas.* (See 1 Corinthians 15:1-4)

Jesus Christ died that man might live. Apart from Him there is no life, either on this earth or in the future. Only Jesus Christ holds out any hope for the sinner (no other religion has a redemptive force, no other religion is redemptive). Only in the Gospel is "the power of God unto salvation for everyone that believes. . ."

Religion is faith in human nature, in what man can do for himself. Religion is man trying to lift himself by his own bootstraps. The futility of religion is obvious on the surface and nothing is more thoroughly evident in history than the fundamental failure of human nature at its best. One contemporary theologian, Karl Barth has said, "Religion is infidelity because it is man's faith in himself."

Christianity is faith in God, in His promises, in His Word, in His Son and the life and words and work of His Son. While speaking in a series of lectures at the Pacific School of Religion to several hundred pastors, Dr. Emil Brunner was asked, "Do you really believe that Jesus Christ is the only way to God?" The great theologian answered, "There is a verse of Scripture which says, 'There is no other name under heaven given among men whereby we must be saved.', do you expect me to quarrel with that?" "The idols of the heathen are silver and gold, the work of man's hands. They have mouths, but they speak not; eyes have they, but they see not; they have ears, but they hear not; neither is there any breath in their mouths. They that make them are like unto them; so is every one that trusteth in them."—Paslm 135:15-18.

****

What explanation does Paul give for the power in the Gospel? What is the characteristic of man's sin as set forth in Romans 1:18-23?

Is Money For Missions
A Poor Economy?

Matthew 28:16-20

Annually the Christian Church spends millions of dollars on its foreign mission's enterprise. The practical question rises, why is such a large amount invested in the foreign mission of the Church? Is it justifiable in the light of present day needs? What is the real justification for missions anyway?

Is it the need of the field? This is important. No Christian can be aware of the desperate plight of the masses of Asia for example, without having some compassion, some desire to help. But this is not the justification for missions.

Is it in order that we may share "our way of life" with the peoples of the world? Hardly, though we may feel our way is best. In many cases western culture has been a destructive force when others have been uprooted from their ancient cultures and have not been taught the roots of our civilization and brought to faith in Christ.

Is it to the end that man's misery might be alle-

214

viated? Worthy as this is as a goal, it falls short of the real incentive of foreign missions.

The plain fact is that there is one overwelming reason for the foreign missions enterprise. That reason is not the need or misery of men, not the propagation of western culture. The one dominating motive for the mission of the Church, the justification for the millions invested in it annually, is that Jesus Christ commanded His Church to do this!

The last thing He said before ascending to the Father (Acts 1:8) was to challenge His Church to be witnesses of the Gospel to the "uttermost parts of the earth." This was His mandate! The Church that does not promote foreign missions with zeal is guilty of disobeying the one thing her Lord commanded her to do. No other justification is necessary, the commission of Jesus Christ is sufficient. We must, if we are to call Him Lord, be everlastingly at the job of telling everybody everywhere of the love of God in Christ. "Ye shall receive power, after that the Holy Spirit is come upon you; and ye shall be witnesses unto me both in Jerusalem, and in all Judea, and in Samaria, and unto the uttermost part of the earth."—Acts 1:8.

❈❈❈❈❈❈❈❈❈❈❈

Some of the most disillusioned missionaries who ever went to the field were those who went for some other reason than obedience to Christ's commission. Worthy as other motives are, they are not adequate to support the morale of the one who goes abroad with serious intentions. Only the highest purpose, obedience to Christ, is sufficient to keep a missionary on the job, come what may, telling the good news. Those who go for lesser reasons either return disillusioned, or settle down into the rut of an average, mediocre ministry, or become professional and hardened or sweat out increasing disappointment and heartbreak as they die a little more each day. Whatever else you do, pray for your missionaries! They really count on your prayer!

The Primary Task Of Missions

1 Corinthians 2:1-5

There are many ways of witnessing to the love of God as it has been given in Jesus Christ. It is hardly worthwhile to speak of God's love to a person if one does not demonstrate that love in his life. In fact, for one to speak of the love of God when his life does not show love can be devastating in its effect upon non-Christians. Perhaps no single thing has alienated as many people from Christ as loveless Christians.

Paul, the Apostle, makes it clear that without love everything else is pointless (1 Corinthians 13). Eloquence, sacrifice, philanthropy, prophecy, martyrdom, faith, mean nothing—they are hollow, transparent, counterfeit, if they are not mixed with love.

God's love is expressed in many ways on the mission field: in the work of healing by medical missions, in the work of charity by the welfare agencies of the Church, in the work of compassion in orphanages, widow's homes, schools for the blind and deaf and crippled, in the work of education and agriculture. But important as these are, they are not primary. Evangelism is the primary task of the mission enterprise. All these others support the primary work. The first great missionary, the Apostle Paul, went out with but one thing, a message. Encountered by Jesus Christ on the road to Damascus, he had been commissioned to proclaim to the gentiles the death and resurrection of Christ. Paul was not disobedient to the heavenly vision. It was this message, ratified by the love and sacrifice of Christians, that turned the Roman Empire upside down in a generation.

Other things are important, and without them the mission of the Church would be incomplete, but evangelism comes first. That is why the pulpit, not the altar, is central in Protestantism. Not the mass, but an open Bible is the center of our worship and service. "It pleased God by the foolishness of preaching to save them that believed."—1 Corinthians 1:21.

❖❖❖❖❖❖❖❖❖❖❖

In the context it is helpful to remember that Paul was not unqualified as a scholar. He had sat at the feet of Israel's greatest teacher, Gamaliel. He was brilliant and logical, as witnessed by his epistles. Yet he did not resort to the wisdom of man in his preaching. Why? What did he fear about human eloquence and human wisdom?

The Power Of The Missionary

Acts 1:4-8

It is indisputable that Jesus Christ was the most captivating, fascinating personality ever to walk the earth. The records of His life indicate that there was a magnetism about Him that drew men to Him in droves. During His public ministry, He was hardly ever free from the multitudes. Even when He deliberately left them and moved to another place, they would follow. His fame was spread abroad.

"No man ever spake like this man," said they of Him. "He speaks, not as the scribes, but as one having authority." "From whence hath this man this learning?" they inquired. One can almost feel the wonder and the awe that covered the crowds as they watched and listened to Him.

Whence this magnetism? Whence this irresistible attraction? Whence the power of His word, the power of His glance?

The secret of His matchless life is not difficult to find. He himself discussed again and again the source of His powerful ministry. He said His words were not His own but the Father's. He insisted His works were not His own but the Father's. Jesus was a man fully yielded, fully owned, fully possessed by God the Holy Spirit! His life was one of strict and explicit obedience to the Father. He was a man filled with the Spirit of God.

Before He ascended to the Father, Jesus said it was to the advantage of His disciples that He go, for when He did, the Comforter, the Holy Spirit would come. He promised the Holy Spirit to the Church and that gift was given on the day of Pentecost (Acts 2). That day, through the Spirit-filled witness of the one hundred and twenty disciples and the preaching of Peter, three thousand Jews were saved and baptized.

Jesus left a mandate to His Church to go into the world, beginning at home, to preach the Gospel. And He left His Church the power to carry out the mandate. He sent the Holy Spirit to be the power. He committed to His Church the ministry of reconciliation and He gave His Church the Holy Spirit to enable her to fulfill the ministry. The commission is binding on every Christian, and the Holy Spirit is available to every Christian.

The Holy Spirit is the power of the Christian witness, the Christian mission. Whether it is the missionary actively engaged in evangelism on the field, or the layman, faithfully witnessing in his community or on his job, the power of the witness is the same, the Holy Spirit. "If you then, being evil, know how to give good gifts unto your children; how much more shall your heavenly Father give the Holy Spirit to them that ask Him?"—Luke 11:13.

❖❖❖❖❖❖❖❖❖❖❖

It is impossible to overestimate the importance of the word "after" in Acts 1:8. Take some time to think on this verse with this in mind. As you think about it, what is the strength of the word "after"? What is the one condition which must obtain before one is able to witness?

CHAPTER EIGHT

The Mature Man

Do You Have A View?

Psalm 121

It makes all the difference in the world where a man looks! Keep your eye on the road fifteen feet ahead of your car and your driving will be erratic. Look out ahead a hundred feet—two hundred—and feel yourself steady at the wheel. There are times when a man needs to look away from the immediate and set his gaze on the horizon. It reminds him that there is more to life than his own little busy world. One harried executive used to swing around in his chair and spend five minutes looking at the skyline through his office window. He found this to be a good antidote for fuzzy thinking. Thoughts began to fall into place, facts began to line up in the order of their importance. He got out from under confusion and was able to be objective about things.

The Psalmist knew the secret. Setting his eyes on the hills, he was reminded Who made them, and he knew that his help came from the same source.

DO YOU HAVE A VIEW?

The strong silence of the solitary hills spoke peace
to his distraught soul as he was reminded that the
God of the hills was also his God, utterly dependable and unfailing.

❖❖❖❖❖❖❖❖❖❖❖❖

How puny my little trials seem against the back-
ground of God's mighty handiwork. Trouble is, I
can get tangled up in the web of my circumstances
if I fail to look away at the reminder of His om-
nipotence. The Psalmist was completely confident
in the guidance of God (verse 8).

Three Sides To Every Question

1 Corinthians 13

There are three sides to every question, not just two sides. Your side, the other fellow's side, and the right side. The only real cure for any problem is to discover the right side. This is the crux of the matter—we are not really interested in the right side. We are interested in our side, the other fellow is interested in his side. Result is impasse, deadlock. Deadlocks are resolved only by concession and expedience.

The real issue is lost in foolish finagling, plotting, scheming, and the whole system moves along on a lower, instead of a higher level. Like little boys on a vacant lot, "I won't let you use my ball unless you let me pitch." You don't get the best pitcher that way! And each side harbors grudges, regrets concessions it has been forced to make, burns with resentment deep down inside. Like a volcano resentments seethe, smolder, someday to erupt in worse conflagration.

THREE SIDES TO EVERY QUESTION

Here's a husband and wife not getting along. He has his side, she hers. Neither wants to give in, until finally they are forced to out of sheer necessity, in order to live together. So concessions are made. Each one reluctantly gives in part way, neither can quite forget, each feels he is right. Then some silly little argument sets it off again, worse than before. Buried grudges explode to the surface, driving them wider and wider apart until divorce is all that is left. There is a third side to that! The right side. God's side. It is the only possible remedy. It would work, if each would take that side. That would settle it once for all and lift the whole thing to a new level.

Here is conflict in industry. Management has its side, labor too. Each fights to maintain its "rights." Deadlock! Then they begin to whittle, jockey, conspire, finally agree, but with each side giving in as little as necessary, cutting in on the other as much as possible. Both cherish the day they can regain what they lost in concessions granted out of sheer expediency. The problem is not solved, just postponed. Resentments burn quietly, deeply, explosively.

Expediency will never cure. It only stops the headache temporarily, lets the disease run its course. We need clean, sharp, final solutions. We must learn to seek the right side to every question, home, business, industry, nation, world. There is no alternative but chaos! What is saner than both sides of an argument agreeing that the right way is best for both, then seeking the right way together for mutual benefit. "Submit yourselves one to another in reverence for God."—Ephesians 5:21. (R.S.V.)

❖❖❖❖❖❖❖❖❖❖❖

Does love sound sentimental in terms of industrial conflicts? Read 1 Corinthians through again, familiarize yourself with the practical, wise, comprehensive strategy of love. It gets results!

Is Your God Big Enough?

Psalm 136

How big is your God?

The measure of Christian effectiveness is not the measure of a man's faith, but the God of his faith. Not our faith, but God's faithfulness is the clue to power and efficiency. The plain fact is that some people are ineffective, not because they do not try, but because they are unfamiliar with the God Who is revealed in the Bible. To put it another way, "their God is too small."

One of the symptoms of what is called "original sin" is man's tendency to whittle God down to man's size. We don't think of it this way of course, but we're doing it a great deal. This is the contradiction in sin. This is the irrational inclination in man which results from sin. The Bible declares that man was made "in the image of God." *Sin makes man want to make God in the image of man.*

This perversion is more apparent when you observe how men tend to build themselves up by tearing somebody else down. Unable to rise above the crowd any other way, some men belittle those who have, and thus try to get on top. Of course it doesn't really work, it only serves to expose the littleness in the man who tries it. Neither does it work to belittle God. It may cater to intellectual pride, but it leaves a man bankrupt in other ways. No man can be bigger than his God.

Big God—big men . . . little God—little men . . . no God—hollow men!

The key to maximum personal triumph in life is an awareness of the complete integrity and adequacy of God. No consideration could be more profitable for a man than this. "Great is the Lord, and greatly to be praised; and His greatness is unsearchable."— Psalm 145:3

✤✤✤✤✤✤✤✤✤✤✤

One way to appreciate the Psalms is to read them aloud. You will find this especially true of Psalm 136. Read it aloud to yourself, as well as to your family or friends, you'll find it will do something for you. It will lift your sights, give you an overview of life that will be exhilarating. Psalm 136 is excellent to read when you are "down in the dumps" or "under the circumstances."

The Mighty God

Isaiah 40:18-31

The Bible does not attempt to prove God. It begins with God—takes God for granted. So much so, in fact, that the Bible declares a man to be irrational who denies God ("The fool hath said in his heart, 'There is no God.' "). Stop to think about it, it is ridiculous to try to prove God—like trying to prove infinity or eternity. You can't prove absolutes. You can't get God in a test tube or under a microscope . . . or even in a telescope. The Bible never falls victim to the presumptuous task of trying to prove God. The Bible declares God to be a fact! The fact is obvious—except to the fool!

This does not mean that God will prove Himself. God does not make Himself hard to find or to know or to love. Indeed, the Bible speaks of a God Who is constantly taking the initiative toward man. "God hath not left Himself without a witness" declares the Apostle (Acts 14:17). God witnesses to Himself in nature, in history, in the human heart. He witnesses to Himself in the Bible and pre-eminently in His Son, Jesus Christ. The evidence is overwhelming—the evidence to the contrary is trivial—but God can do nothing for the man who refuses to consider the evidence, who obstinately turns his back upon the loving overtures of the heavenly Father.

The prophets knew God, and in this passage Isaiah gives an eloquent description of the God whom the prophets served. He is a big God! He is omniscient (knows everything), omnipotent (all powerful), and omnipresent (everywhere at once). How does your God measure up to the God of the Bible? "The Lord is the strength of my life; of whom shall I be afraid?"—Psalm 27:1.

❖❖❖❖❖❖❖❖❖❖❖

There are many kinds of idols—the kind Isaiah describes in this passage for example. Modern, civilized man would not think of serving idols such as Isaiah mentions, but he has his idols. *Whatever a man puts first in life is his god—his idol.* Who is your God? What is most important to you?

What Is God Like?

John 14:5-14

What is God like? Through the centuries men have struggled to find the answer to that question. And far too often their quest ended in failure and despair. Men realize instinctively that it is important to know God—they never seriously doubt that God is there, somewhere, but where? How can God be found? How can He be known?

Of course there have been those in every generation who have totally disregarded the abundant evidence on every hand and denied the existence of God. This is interesting, because if there were no God to deny, the arguments of the atheist would be ridiculous and laughable. No one would take him seriously. The only thing that saves the atheist's self-respect is the fact that there is a God against Whom his struggle is real! The atheist is not shadow boxing. If God did not exist, the atheist would not be taken any more seriously than a man who vociferously tried to prove there is no Santa Claus.

God is there to be sure. No one honest with himself in his heart will deny this. But where? And what is God like? Many, failing to find God outside themselves, invent a god. But this invention has never been quite satisfactory. After all, it doesn't make sense for a man to bow down and worship that which he himself creates.

The New Testament has a clear answer to this question, and multiplied millions through the ages have discovered that God is no mystery at all. He can be known, He can be as real as a friend. The answer is Jesus Christ. God is like Jesus! *Get to know Jesus Christ, you'll find that God is a reality in your experience.*

This is not something to argue about! This is something to be experienced. As long as men insist on arguing with Jesus Christ, they will never get to know God. But if a man will honestly try Jesus Christ, he will be in for the most important discovery of his life.

Contrary to a rather common misconception, the disciples of Jesus were not "sucked in" by Jesus. They did not come easily to faith in Him. They felt the pressure of the opposition and undoubtedly entertained many doubts triggered by the arguments of Jesus' enemies. The disciples themselves had many questions which they did not hesitate to ask.

And incidentally, Jesus never dodged a question, or passed the buck. However, there were certain facts that were simply indisputable. Even the opposition could not deny this. The facts stood and no man in his right mind could ignore them, least of all, those who found Jesus to be thoroughly consistent in His life. They followed Him, not so much because they understood Him, but as they were compelled by the irresistible facts of His integrity, His teaching and His deeds. "To as many as received Him, to them He gave the power to become the sons of God . . ."—John 1:12.

❖❖❖❖❖❖❖❖❖❖

What can a man lose by really allowing Christ to prove His reality? If He is not God, this will soon be apparent and having the matter settled one way or the other will give some satisfaction. The trouble is that some who read this will keep Jesus at arm's length with academic arguments which deceive only their inventors, and will not dare to ask Christ, if He is real, to make God known to them. If a man really wants to know God, and will ask Jesus Christ to help him, he will not be disappointed, that's for sure! Note verses 7-9.

Faith Is Possession

John 15:1-7

Christianity is more than profession . . . it is possession! A possession which works two ways: The Christian possesses Christ and Christ possesses the Christian. "Christ in you, the hope of glory," declares Paul. That's possessing Christ. Again he says, "Now you are in Christ Jesus." That's being possessed by Christ. This double-barreled possession is Christian reality—anything less is a caricature.

Each man ought to settle this question for himself: Do I possess Christ? Does Christ possess me? Mere profession of certain dogmas, however sound —mere application of certain ethical precepts, however virtuous, are a far cry from bona-fide, authentic Christianity. To be a Christian is to possess and be possessed by Jesus Christ. To have Christ is to have all one needs for time and eternity. To be Christ's is the absolute assurance of personal fulfillment—the assurance of becoming the man

God intended you to be—the man you long to be at your best.

"I beseech you therefore brethren, by the mercies of God, to present your body a living sacrifice, wholly, acceptable unto God, which is your reasonable service . . ."—Romans 12:1.

❋❋❋❋❋❋❋❋❋❋❋❋

What is the relationship between the vine and the branches? Where does the life to produce fruit come from? What does "abide" mean? How does one do it?

Know Your Assets

Ephesians 3:14-21

Christians fail, not because they do not try, but because they do not make use of their assets. Being unfamiliar with the resources God has made available, or failing to draw upon them when needed, many a person limps along the best he can on his own limited resources. His Christian life is a pale, thin, shallow imitation of the real thing.

The Christian life is not difficult, it is impossible. Only Christ can live it! The essence of the Christian experience is that Christ literally indwells a man, working in and through him God's will and purpose. The man who struggles in his human best to act like a Christian, suffers either the pride of partial or sporadic success, or the despair of aggravating failure, if he does not drift along on a dismal plateau of mediocrity, indifference and apathy.

God does not leave a man to his own devices to attain righteousness. In Christ God has provided all any man needs to be everything He requires! The effective person, recognizing his own inadequacy, enjoys confidence in the sufficiency of God's grace in Christ and by faith draws upon that supply continually as he draws upon the atmosphere for oxygen. Christian growth is a matter of learning the necessity of dependence upon Christ within. The first step in drawing upon the resources is to recognize that they are actually available. Obviously if a man is unaware of his assets, he will not make use of them. He might as well be without help if he does not know it is present.

This is the burden of Paul's prayer in this passage. He is anxious that the Ephesians know the more-than-sufficient provision God has made. This provision is made known in the Bible. For this reason a man needs to get acquainted with the Bible, not simply for the sake of knowing about it, but that he may be aware of his spiritual assets. The wise Christian is as regular in his use of the Bible as he is in other habits which are basic to health and strength. The Apostle Peter puts it this way, "Whereby are given unto us exceeding great and precious promises, that by these ye might be partakers of the divine nature, having escaped the corruption that is in the world through lust."—2 Peter 1:4. The Bible might be compared to a bank book which carries a record of the "deposit" God has made in Christ to meet every need of man in his daily living and growth in grace. The big question is, are you familiar with your deposit book?

✦✦✦✦✦✦✦✦✦✦✦✦

Notice that Paul prays that the "inner man" might be strengthened, what is the source of that strength? How does Christ dwell in the heart? Make a list of the different things for which Paul prays. Notice the promise in verse 20.

Absolute Safety

John 6:35-40

Security is legitimate only when it is a by-product of a nobler goal. Apart from Jesus Christ, security and freedom lie at opposite poles. As a man demands security, he sacrifices freedom, and vice versa. (You can't steal second base without taking your foot off first.) Security at any price leads inevitably to slavery. Except in Christ! In Christ security and freedom meet. The man in Christ enjoys maximum security and maximum freedom. The man in Christ simply cannot lose. The past is covered by Christ's sacrifice, the future is in the hands of Him Who "knows the end from the beginning" and Whose guidance is infallible, and for the present God promises,"My grace is sufficient for thee," and "as thy day, so shall thy strength be."

Jesus Christ guarantees a man absolute safety—absolute freedom! Apart from Jesus Christ both are an illusion. "Truly, truly, I say to you, every one who commits sin is a slave to sin. The slave does not continue in the house forever; the son continues forever. So if the Son makes you free, you will be free indeed."—John 8:34-36.

❖❖❖❖❖❖❖❖❖❖❖

What do you think it means to be "in Christ?" Professor James Stewart of Scotland says, "To be in Christ means that Christ is the redeemed man's environment." Where does one find security outside of Jesus Christ?

Built To Take It!

Hebrews 12:1-6

It is what's inside a man that counts in the pinches. How he takes the emergency, how he meets the crisis, depends upon inner resources. Muscle may pay off in a brawl, but in adversity it is less than useless. The bigger the man, the harder he falls if he counts on brawn when life tumbles in. Courage is not in the biceps, it is in the heart. Whether a man cracks up or rebounds under pressure, depends upon a resiliency which only spiritual vitality can give.

To get a picture of men who could take it, read the last part of the eleventh chapter of Hebrews beginning at the 32nd verse. Unlike the victories of faith recorded in the first part of the chapter, these heroes really took a beating, but their strength was in the Lord, and they were more than conquerors. It is these triumphant ones the author of Hebrews has in mind as he moves into the twelfth chapter and speaks about "so great a cloud of witnesses."

The man who starves his soul is usually a pushover in the crisis. Either he takes an escape, or he collapses, or he whines and lets himself be eaten out with self-pity. He pays a terrible price when he neglects his soul, depriving himself of spiritual resources so abundantly available. He is like a man living on a dwindling capital.

But that man is invincible who nourishes his soul regularly on the Word of God. Calamity may strike, but spiritual resources make him invulnerable. He rides the waves in a crisis instead of being swamped by them. Happy the man who has discovered that the real enemy is within and that Jesus Christ is the only adequate defense. Such a man is the master, never the victim of circumstances, no matter how black or tragic or unexpected they may be. "In all these things (trials, troubles, dangers, reverses, failures, etc.) we are more than conquerors through Him Who loved us . . ."—Romans 8:37.

❖❖❖❖❖❖❖❖❖❖❖

The author admonishes the Christian to do three things in verses one and two which qualify a man for victory, but even more important is the consideration he urges in verse three.

The Profit In Patience

Isaiah 40:28-31

Sometimes the most important thing a man can do is wait! It's the most difficult, but always by far the wisest strategy. God's will involves a schedule as well as a purpose to be accomplished. *Submission to His schedule is as important as surrender to His purpose.*

Timing in anything is basic. Take cooking for instance. The good chef takes time seriously. He doesn't want a half-baked product. He doesn't leave a thing in the oven too long either. Whether it's cooking or comedy, drama or real life, timing is fundamental. Acting on impulse is wrong, failing to act because of fear is just as wrong. The balance is learning to wait on God, to let God lead.

The impulsive man gets an idea, runs off half-cocked in all directions and leaves behind a string of half-baked projects. Disregarding Divine guidance he whips up a storm, pushes the panic button, gets things in motion, then lets them peter out. He majors in starting things, fails at the finish, and leaves life cluttered up with a lot of loose ends. He calls it faith, but he's really operating on presumption.

Just as bad is the lazy or fearful or faithless man who never starts anything (he figures he can't fail if he doesn't try) and lets his ideas burn out to ashes. The man who waits on God enjoys the perfection of Divine timing and completion. Question is, when does a man wait, and how long does he wait? What tips him off to action?

The first thing to remember is that when God gives a vision, God Himself will fulfill it! He will use the man, but God by His Holy Spirit is the animation, the dynamic. The man who waits for God to act in Him will be the most active, the most involved in the operation. God may use different means to guide a man, but in the final analysis, the guidance is inward, intuitive. By His indwelling Spirit, God frees or binds, releases or checks. The man who waits on God becomes sensitive to the inner voice.

Got a good idea? Think it is born of God? Give it back to Him, wait reflectively, prayerfully, quietly. *You never waste any time waiting on God!* As long as there is doubt, don't! God will never let you wait too long, never let you miss the signal to go ahead, if you are waiting on Him. Trust Him and you will be surprised how clearly He directs in the right way at the right time. "Wait, I say, on the Lord!"

❖❖❖❖❖❖❖❖❖❖❖

But a man will say, "How do I know I'm really waiting on God? Maybe I'm just scared, or weak? That is a possibility, but you determine whether or not you are waiting on God with your will, not your emotions. You may not feel like you're waiting on God, but you can decide to wait on Him, and this is what God looks at. God doesn't go by your feelings, He goes by your choices!

The Praying Man

Luke 11:1-13

"No atheists in fox holes" was a familiar statement during World War II. It may not always be true, but the fact remains that it was not an uncommon thing to see a tough fighting man pray instinctively under pressure though he may have disregarded or ridiculed prayer when the going was easy. Plenty of men testify to the surprise they experienced when they found themselves praying in a tight spot, inasmuch as they had always figured prayer was "for the birds."

Nothing unusual about this! Man was made for fellowship with God. His spirit demands the atmosphere of heaven just as his body needs the oxygen of earth. Of course a man can neglect his relationship with the heavenly Father and seem to be getting along nicely, but actually, his soul is drying up within him. Trouble is, he may not be aware of this spiritual dry-rot until it is too late.

The best man Who ever lived needed prayer, not just as a religious exercise, but as a steady, continual, unceasing practice. Prayer was not optional with Jesus, it was mandatory. Not that He prayed involuntarily, but that He needed to maintain an around-the-clock contact with His heavenly Father. He was never out of touch, whatever the circumstances, and often He would retire to the hills alone to spend hours, or all night in prayer, or He would arise a great while before the dawn to meet His heavenly Father in a rendezvous of prayer. If Jesus needed to pray, how much more the Christian? "Man ought always to pray, and never stop . . ."—Luke 18:1.

✦✦✦✦✦✦✦✦✦✦✦

Consider the fact that of all the things the disciples might have asked Jesus to teach them, the one thing they wanted to learn was prayer. Why was this? Was it because they realized everything else about Him was due to His prayer life? This passage gives Jesus' lesson on prayer at the request of His disciples. What do you learn about prayer from it?

The Cure For Worry

Philippians 4:1-7

How does a man handle anxiety? If it is not nipped in the bud, it can send a man to the hospital. It takes very little anxiety to cut into his efficiency and take the edge off all he tries to do.

The Christian cure is found in verses 6 and 7. The word "careful" should be translated "anxious" —the meaning it conveyed in the Old English. Everyone agrees that worry is futile and unprofitable. Nothing is accomplished by it. In fact, it increases rather than diminishes the problem. It is easy enough to agree with this in principle, but how does a man stop worrying?

Basically two things cause worry: Failure in the past and uncertainty in the future. Both are beyond man's control. But they are not beyond God's control! This is the key to Christian imperturbability. Past failure is covered by God's foregiveness on the grounds of Christ's sacrifice. The future is secure in

God's sustaining grace. Jesus promised His peace to men, a peace the world cannot give nor take away.

You may choose to think about your circumstances, or you may choose to occupy your mind with the sufficiency of God. Do the first, you will worry, do the latter, you will find the peace of God taking over in your life. "Peace I leave with you; my peace I give to you; not as the world gives do I give to you. Let not your hearts be troubled, neither let them be afraid."—John 14:28. (R.S.V.)

✠✠✠✠✠✠✠✠✠✠✠✠

Philippians 4:6 states the conditions for God's peace and verse 7 gives the results which accrue when the conditions are met. Notice especially the emphasis on "thanksgiving." In this context look at Romans 8:28.

Antidote For Escapism

Have you ever tried to run away from God? This Psalm is the record of one man's experience who did. He discovered that he could not get away. Wherever he went, there was God. Not like a tyrant, but like a loving Father, who loved too much to let His beloved son escape. However, it doesn't appear that God put any brakes on this man. He let him go wherever he felt like running. God was just there, that was all. Wherever he went he met God. God did not tie him down or block his path or hinder his running away, He just followed with His love and compassion. It began to dawn on the man that God's pursuit was one of love and personal interest. There was no bondage in it. On the contrary, there was infinite freedom and provision when he woke up to the facts.

The man reveals a degree of human resentment against the wicked who seemed to prosper (verses

19-22) and was honest with God about his anger. Then he realized that this resentment was as evil as the wickedness he was condemning in others, and his prayer of repentance at the end of the Psalm is beautiful. Run from God if you will, but He will pursue you in love. Open your eyes and your heart and you will begin to enjoy the inexhaustible resources He delights in giving you. Don't blame God just because you find it difficult to enjoy another's prosperity. Count your own blessings and it will surprise you what God has done.

✦✦✦✦✦✦✦✦✦✦✦✦

Verses 17 and 18 are most remarkable to ponder. Think of the amazing truth in these verses which suggests that God has you on His mind all the time.

Strength Where It Matters

Ephesians 6:10-20

The mature Christian is under no illusion about his own strength. His confidence is the strength of Christ. Christian victory is not man's best mixed with God's help, but God alone working in and through man and circumstances—bringing divine conquest. The Christian continues to be frustrated until he accepts the fact that even his efforts to behave opposes God's highest and best.

To illustrate, the drowning man who struggles compounds the problems of the life guard and must be rendered unconscious or immobile so that his efforts to save himself will not end in disaster. Imagine the rubber glove deciding it had a few ideas of its own about surgery. Every effort on its part to assist in the operation would represent resistance to the surgeon. So it is with the Christian, he must learn to let God work in him.

Does this then mean that the Christian is passive?

Does he "sit and twiddle his thumbs" while God works? Does he do nothing? The fact is that the man who has learned to depend upon Christ in him is a very active person, active in the right way at the right time. The Christian himself is the instrument, but the strength, the wisdom, the direction comes from within by the power of Christ. The explanation of the Christian dynamic is in its application: one who realizes his inadequacy and is familiar with the promises regarding the strength of Christ that abound in the Bible, admits his need, yields to Christ and trusts that Christ will do what He promised. Result—he really experiences Christ working in him.

Ephesians 6:10-20 is one familiar passage that approaches this matter of the Christian resources in terms of armor for battle. Paul begins by pointing out that we must be strong "in the Lord and in the power of His might" after which he gives the reason for our need of His strength. "Work out your own salvation with fear and trembling, for it is God that worketh in you both to will and to do of His good pleasure."—Philippians 2:12-13.

✤✤✤✤✤✤✤✤✤✤✤✤

From whence does the real opposition of the Christian come? Where does he get the facilities to resist this opposition? What are those facilities?

Future Unlimited

Ephesians 1:3-14

Predestination isn't a bad word! Nor is it a Presbyterian invention. If you take the Bible seriously, you come face to face with it often. It is of the very essence of Scripture.

Predestination is not fatalism. It does not mean "what will happen, will happen . . ." that man is helpless before an inflexible inevitability. It does not mean that freedom is an illusion, that man is a puppet who jumps as God pulls strings. It does not mean that an overpowering, impersonal Deity rides roughshod over His creatures like a steam roller with inexorable force.

Actually, nothing is clearer in Scripture (and experience) than that man is free—and responsible. Man chooses without interference or intimidation . . . and man is aware of the responsibility of his choices.

Predestination does mean that God knows what

He is doing, and that He is able to do it. It means
that He has a plan conceived without consulting
man, which plan is being worked out in history and
cannot fail. It teaches that God is never overcome,
that He is always in charge. He is not fickle or
capricious. He is omnipotent (all-powerful)—omniscient (knows everything)—and immutable (un-
changing).

Furthermore, He is a God of love who takes a
personal, intimate, fatherly interest in each of us.
"For He has made known unto us, in all wisdom and
insight, the mystery of His will, according to His
purpose which He set forth in Christ as a plan for
the fulness of time, to unite all things in Christ . . ."
—Ephesians 1:9-10. (R.S.V.)

"We know that in everything God works for
good with those who love him, who are called according to his purpose. For those whom he fore-
knew he also predestined to be conformed to the
image of his Son, in order that he might be the first-
born among many brethren. And those whom he
predestined he also called; and those whom he called
he also justified; and those whom he justified he also
glorified. What then shall we say to this? If God is
for us, who is against us? He who did not spare his
own Son but gave him up for us all, will he not also
give us all things with him? Who shall bring any
charge against God's elect? It is God who justifies;
who is to condemn? Is it Christ Jesus, who died,

yes, who was raised from the dead, who is at the right hand of God, who indeed intercedes for us? Who shall separate us from the love of Christ? Shall tribulation, or distress, or persecution, or famine, or nakedness, or peril, or sword? As it is written, 'For thy sake we are being killed all the day long; we are regarded as sheep to be slaughtered.' No, in all these things we are more than conquerors through him who loved us. For I am sure that neither death, nor life, nor angels, nor principalities, nor things present, nor things to come, nor powers, nor height, nor depth, nor anything else in all creation, will be able to separate us from the love of God in Christ Jesus our Lord."—Romans 8:28-39 R.S.V.

For a thrilling experiment, write down all the verbs in this passage which describe what God has done in Christ for the believer. What do they add up to?

Acknowledgements

To, Thomas Nelson and Sons, Publishers of New York for permission to quote from the REVISED STANDARD VERSION OF THE BIBLE copyrighted in 1946 and 1952 by the Division of Christian Education, National Council of Churches.

To, The Macmillan Company of New York for permission to quote from THE NEW TESTAMENT IN MODERN ENGLISH by J. B. Phillips.